PREFACE

At the behest of the 24th United States–Republic of Korea (U.S.–ROK) Security Consultative Meeting (SCM) of October 1992, RAND and the Korea Institute of Defense Analyses (KIDA) undertook a joint project to assess whether and how the United States and the ROK can maintain and invigorate their security relationship should North Korea no longer pose a major threat to peace and stability on the Korean peninsula. The two research teams for the project intensively reviewed the past history and present status of the U.S.–ROK alliance, and explored future challenges. As part of a larger review of U.S.–ROK security relations mandated by the U.S. Secretary of Defense and the ROK Minister of National Defense, RAND and KIDA pursued three broad research objectives:

- To identify and analyze the principal characteristics of and potential directions for long-term U.S.–ROK security cooperation

- To define a policy framework and criteria with which both countries could evaluate the suitability, feasibility, and consequences of alternative forms of security cooperation under shifting peninsular and regional conditions

- To highlight emerging policy issues that the study teams believe both governments will need to address in planning for the future.

The SCM is the principal annual U.S.–ROK security planning meeting, jointly chaired by the U.S. Secretary of Defense and the ROK Minister of National Defense, and is attended by other senior defense officials from both countries. It is convened to review ongoing issues in the U.S.–ROK alliance, to achieve consensus on measures that the two governments are to undertake jointly, and to identify pertinent policy questions that warrant further consideration and consultation.

This report summarizes the results of that collaborative research project, "Shaping the Future U.S.–Korean Security Relationship." It draws on numerous project briefings and working papers prepared over the course of the research. It also draws on formal briefings presented by the leaders of the RAND and KIDA teams to several major bilateral planning meetings, which included the U.S.–ROK Policy Review Subcommittee (PRS) meetings in August 1993 and August 1994, and the 26th SCM in October 1994. At the 26th SCM, the project results and recommendations were presented to the U.S. Secretary of Defense and the ROK Minister of National Defense.

This document reflects the individual and collective contributions of the twelve members of the RAND and KIDA research teams. Jonathan Pollack, senior adviser for International Policy at RAND, served as the RAND research team leader. Young Koo Cha (then a senior research fellow at KIDA and at present the deputy director of the Policy Planning Office of the ROK Ministry of National Defense) served as the KIDA team leader. The two team leaders were jointly responsible for the preparation of this report, but its content is the product of intensive interactions among various team members. The other RAND team members included Norman Levin, senior staff member, International Policy; Richard Kugler and Donald Henry, senior staff members, Washington Research Department; Admiral James Winnefeld (Ret.), senior consultant, Washington Research Department; and Kongdan Oh, former staff member, International Policy. The other KIDA team members included Changsu Kim, senior research fellow; Chai-Ki Sung, Choon-Il Chung, and Choo-Suk Suh, research fellows; and Du-Hyeogn Cha, associate research fellow.

In addition, LTCs Richard Curasi and Michael Baier (while serving successively as visiting U.S. Army fellows at KIDA) participated in some of the project discussions and joint research workshops. Yong-Sup Han (then assistant to the ROK Minister of National Defense and now professor at the Korean National Defense College) contributed on a consulting basis during the initial phases of project research.

RAND's participation in the project was sponsored by the Office of Asia-Pacific Affairs of the Assistant Secretary of Defense for International Security Affairs. RAND's efforts were conducted under the International Security and Defense Policy Center of RAND's National Defense Research Institute, a federally funded research and development center sponsored by the Office of the Secretary of Defense, the Joint Staff, and the defense agencies.

This document seeks both to assist the U.S. and ROK governments in their deliberations about the future of the security relationship and to stimulate broader public debate. The opinions and judgments it contains represent those of the authors and do not reflect the official policies of either the U.S. or ROK government.

A NEW ALLIANCE
FOR THE NEXT CENTURY
The Future of U.S.–Korean Security Cooperation

Jonathan D. Pollack
Young Koo Cha

WITH

Changsu Kim, Richard L. Kugler,
Chai-Ki Sung, Norman D. Levin, Choon-Il Chung,
James A. Winnefeld, Choo-Suk Suh,
Donald P. Henry, Du-Hyeogn Cha,
Kongdan Oh

National Defense Research Institute

Prepared for the
Office of the Secretary of Defense

RAND

CONTENTS

FIGURES

ASSESSING AN ALLIANCE

RAND and the Korea Institute of Defense Analyses (KIDA) undertook a joint project to assess whether and how the United States and the Republic of Korea (ROK) can maintain and invigorate their security relationship should North Korea no longer pose a major threat to peace and stability on the Korean peninsula. The two research teams for the project intensively reviewed the past history and present status of the U.S.–ROK alliance, and explored future challenges. In this context, *alliance* denotes a host of interrelated policy understandings and agreements that, when fully developed, include

- a strategic concept defining the shared obligations of alliance partners

- a defense strategy through which the roles and responsibilities of each partner are specified

- an agreement on types and levels of forces to implement a common defense strategy

- a range of more-specialized agreements on command relations, base arrangements, and burden-sharing.

The primary value of the project was in the candid exchange of ideas and the building of a working consensus, which enabled both research teams to focus on the major challenges of transition and transformation that the U.S.–ROK alliance is likely to face in future years. Thus, a single policy document cannot capture all the richness and detail of the deliberations, especially because, in synthesizing and integrating the judgments of two research teams, both simplification and exclusion were required.

Many of the pivotal factors that first prompted the creation of the U.S.–ROK alliance have undergone profound change, even though North Korea remains avowedly hostile to the well-being and security of the Republic of Korea:

- The Soviet Union has disintegrated. With its demise, the bipolar confrontation between it and the United States as superpowers has ended.

- The ROK is no longer a vulnerable and underdeveloped society, and the overall power balance on the peninsula continues to shift in the ROK's favor.

- The region as a whole has experienced sustained economic and political development, transforming highly dependent relationships between the United States and its regional allies into much more symmetrical and balanced ones.

- Russia and China have reached a growing economic and political accommodation with the ROK, thereby diminishing some of the principal threats to Korean security.

In this report, we describe analyses undertaken at the behest of the 24th U.S.–ROK Security Consultative Meeting (SCM) of October 1992, and as part of a larger review of U.S.–ROK security relations mandated by the U.S. Secretary of Defense and the ROK Minister of National Defense. The SCM is the principal annual U.S.–ROK security planning meeting, jointly chaired by the U.S. Secretary of Defense and the ROK Minister of National Defense, and is attended by other senior defense officials from both countries. It is convened to review ongoing issues in the U.S.–ROK alliance, to achieve consensus on measures that the two governments are to undertake jointly, and to identify pertinent policy questions that warrant further consideration and consultation.

The analyses derive from a detailed and rigorous assessment by the two research teams of prospective changes in the alliance. Such changes could stem either from shifts in relations between North and South Korea, from changes in the larger regional security context, or from both. The study's findings build directly on assessments and expert judgment structured along the following major dimensions:

• Four alternative models of the future U.S.–ROK security relationship

• An evaluation of each security alternative according to three time periods, or *phases*, that represent shifting peninsular conditions—*status quo*, accommodation and integration, and post-unification

• Specified criteria for evaluating the suitability, feasibility, and flexibility of various changes in security relations

• Four posited transition paths that would lead to different longer-term policy outcomes and end states in the U.S.–ROK security relationship, each positing different levels of future policy integration.

CONFRONTING SECURITY POLICY CHALLENGES

The United States and the Republic of Korea confront three principal policy challenges at present: (1) ensuring that the combined deterrence and defense capabilities of the two countries remain fully in place so long as North Korea poses a major danger to peninsular stability; (2) achieving the transition in South-North relations envisioned in the December 1991 Agreement on Reconciliation, Non-aggression, Exchanges and Cooperation Between the South and the North (otherwise referred to as the Basic Agreement) and in the December 1991 Joint Declaration of the Denuclearization of the Korean Peninsula; and (3) developing and articulating a logic for future security collaboration, assuming diminution of the North Korean threat and the ultimate unification of the Korean peninsula.

IDENTIFYING SECURITY ALTERNATIVES

To identify potential models of security alternatives for meeting these challenges, the two teams focused on three principal questions:

- What are the discernible models of security cooperation between the United States and the ROK, at present and in the future?

- What are the principal characteristics of collaboration—specific strategic concepts and operational dimensions—under each alternative?

- Under what circumstances—transitional events—would each security arrangement be most relevant to the two countries?

RAND and KIDA focused on four principal alternatives that comprise varying answers to these questions: (1) a robust peninsular alliance, (2) a reconfigured peninsular alliance, (3) a regional security alliance, and (4) a political alliance. Each alternative required that the two research teams provide separate assessments of the peninsular security situation, the primary focus of security cooperation between the two countries, and the obligations and security conditions for that alternative.

EVALUATING SECURITY ALTERNATIVES

To gauge the four security alternatives more fully, the two teams assessed how those alternatives might function across a range of futures, in the context of different policy needs that the United States and the ROK could face in the coming decade. This approach enabled RAND and KIDA to specify a number of possible conditions, then to consider what demands those conditions might impose on both states. The two research teams devised organizing concepts around which specific policy alternatives could be subjected to more-detailed evaluation. Two steps proved especially crucial: (1) identifying the operative political and security circumstances on the peninsula, as designated by the three phases described above, that were most conducive to a particular security alternative; and (2) specifying criteria for measuring the appropriateness of the security alternatives to the interests and strategies of both countries.

The three major criteria were defined as follows: *Suitability* denotes appropriateness for achieving the most important policy objectives shared by both countries. *Feasibility* concerns the domestic support in both states for pursuing shared alliance goals, and the capacity of both countries to pursue collaborative ends without incurring adverse effects from any of the ROK's neighbors. *Flexibility* points to the major failures in policy that both countries hope to avoid but cannot preclude under all circumstances. The RAND and KIDA evaluations differed most over the feasibility criterion, which characterizes the domestic views of the security relationship. Those differences highlight how crucial the management of security cooperation is within a domestic context: The differences grew more marked as concerns about the immediacy of the North Korean threat diminished and as the separate domestic publics were more likely to voice increased sentiment for renegotiating the terms of the security relationship. The desire of both leaderships (but especially the United States') for ensuring alliance effectiveness (including high degrees of interoperability in weapon systems) could come into conflict with the domestic desires in the ROK for enhancing Korea's decisionmaking autonomy. These desires include expectations that overall defense costs will be reduced, that the ROK's contributions to alliance burden-sharing will be reduced equivalently, and that the flow of U.S. defense technology to the ROK will be increased.

For a more-detailed evaluation, the two research teams then rank-ordered the four specific policy alternatives according to how they met combinations of the three phases and subcriteria of the three main criteria, as shown in Figure S.1 (where "1" indicates highest rank). The final scores were intended principally for illustrative purposes; the numbers should not be interpreted as being precise.

Both research teams strongly favored maintaining a robust peninsular alliance so long as North Korea continues its hostility and offensive military deployments against the ROK. Should political and military conditions in Korea move in a more positive direction, both teams substantially favored a regional security alliance—promoting U.S.–ROK roles and responsibilities beyond the peninsula, either together or in collaboration with other U.S. allies and regional security partners. A reconfigured peninsular alliance, in which the United States would provide principally a rapid-reinforcement capability if a crisis with North Korea recurs, also assumes greater relevance if accommodation and integration occur. But neither research team's findings suggest appreciable support for a purely political alliance, in which the United States and the ROK would be restricted to largely symbolic forms of security cooperation (for example, high-level

RAND *MR594-S.1*

Preferred Alternative, by Phase

	Robust Peninsular Alliance		Reconfigured Peninsular Alliance		Regional Security Alliance		Political Alliance	
	KIDA	RAND	KIDA	RAND	KIDA	RAND	KIDA	RAND
Phase 1: *Status Quo*	**1**	**1**	3	3	2	2	4	4
Phase 2: Accommodation/ Integration	3	2	2	3	**1**	**1**	4	4
Phase 3: Post-Unification	4	3	2	2	**1**	**1**	3	4

Figure S.1—Rank-Ordering the RAND and KIDA Assessments

political consultations, but with minimal security coordination and virtually no peacetime combined defense planning). The two states therefore need to focus on handling two possible transition challenges: how to deal with the uncertainty and potential instability in the period between confrontation and unification, and how to develop future-oriented strategies that would enable full transition to a new security concept once unification takes place.

EXAMINING TRANSITION PATHS

How can the United States and the Republic of Korea most effectively manage the dual transition in security cooperation—first, from an era of high threat to peninsular integration and, second, from integration to a more regionally based strategic concept? To explore these issues, we assessed security-cooperation alternatives and phases that affect the main factors of the alliance relationship.

The post-unification phase will require specification of the goal or the *end state* of the alliance (representing the basic structure underlying security cooperation and different levels of integration and policy coordination). Between the present relationship and that of post-unification, the alliance could follow a number of different paths. The teams judged three of the security alternatives to be conceivable end states: (1) a reconfigured peninsular alliance, (2) one or another variant of a regional security alliance, or (3) a political alliance that assumes a largely autonomous Korea. In the judgment of the two teams, there are four principal transition processes, or *paths*, for longer-term security cooperation between the United States and Korea, diagrammed in Figure S.2. For each of the four paths, we assumed that a robust peninsular alliance remains in place under *status quo* conditions. Beyond that point, however, the paths diverge.

The paths traverse interests and strategies so complex and diverse that the research teams do not believe there is a single optimal model for the future. But both countries need to carefully assess the strengths and weaknesses of different paths, or approaches, and to signal to their domestic publics and to the other countries of East

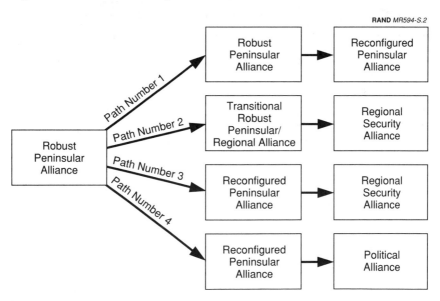

Figure S.2—Four Principal Paths for Long-Term U.S.–Korean Security Cooperation

Asia their shared intention and determination to sustain close security cooperation in the post-unification era.

CONCLUSIONS AND POLICY RECOMMENDATIONS

Defining a post-unification alliance strategy, therefore, represents a central policy challenge for both countries. The long history of interdependence between the two countries will not by itself sustain collaboration if the North Korean threat diminishes appreciably or if unification takes place. There is a parallel risk that without appropriate regard for higher-level strategic concerns (for example, preventing the rise of a hostile hegemon or countering nuclear proliferation), security cooperation will prove more contentious within both countries or could become mired in policy disputes of a lesser order (for example, disputes over defense burden-sharing formulas). Both research teams believe the potential for a post-unification alliance clearly exists, but that such an alliance will require a very different logic and structure from those of the threat-based environment of the Cold War.

A future-oriented alliance would build on past cooperation between the United States and Korea and between the United States and its other major regional allies. A continued commitment to pursue complementary policy goals will help keep potential areas of political, economic, and security divergence in check while also keeping both countries focused on areas of common interest. The two teams also believe that sustained policy interdependence will maximize the security gains for both countries far more than will opting for independent paths without regard for each other's vital interests. Both would gain equally, and neither would enjoy unilateral advantage.

Such a "profit-generating" alliance would help realize the primary policy and security needs of both countries:

- Peninsular stability and security would be achieved at more acceptable cost to both states than under pursuit of independent strategies, and in a manner that benefited their respective interests.

- The unification process would be more effectively managed, with less possibility of costly, highly disruptive outcomes.

- Both states would contribute to regional stability and security commensurate with their capabilities and interests.

- The two countries would jointly enhance peacekeeping capabilities in conjunction with other regional actors.

- The two countries would retain clear incentives to enhance their economic and political interactions in ways beneficial to both.

Without the commitment to build a new alliance, all these goals could be undermined or imperiled outright.

Alliance-building for the post-unification era will require careful, long-term planning and much effort by the political and military leaderships of the United States and the ROK. In the transition process, both countries must adapt existing security arrangements to new requirements, which will involve meshing areas where each enjoys comparative advantage. In addition, both states must be prepared, on an equitable basis, to dedicate forces to roles and responsibilities beyond an exclusively peninsular focus. Even as the two leaderships seek to define the purposes and policy directions underlying future security collaboration, they must build domestic support within the ROK and the United States for pursuing such goals. Without such support, close security cooperation will not be sustainable over the longer term. Equally important, both countries need to ensure that their future security policies and defense programs are fully congruent with one another and are not seen as a threat to any of the ROK's neighbors.

The process of planning for the longer term must begin now, rather than when abrupt or unanticipated change takes place on the peninsula. Planning for the future will demonstrate that both states have an intrinsic interest in sustaining security cooperation, with or without a North Korean threat. Doing so will help ensure that both countries continue to regard close security consultations as integral to their bilateral relationship while bearing in mind the longer-term challenges of peace and stability in a region of abiding interest to the United States as well as to the ROK.

ACKNOWLEDGMENTS

The project leaders (Jonathan D. Pollack and Young Koo Cha) owe a collective debt to all members of the RAND and the Korea Institute of Defense Analyses (KIDA) research teams. They want to acknowledge the particular contributions of Norman Levin, Changsu Kim, and Choon-Il Chung in Chapter Two; Richard Kugler and Chai-Ki Sung in Chapter Three; and James Winnefeld, Choo-Suk Suh, and Du-Hyeogn Cha in Chapter Four.

The final version of the report reflects the incisive critiques of two formal reviewers (Thomas McNaugher of RAND and Paul Bracken of Yale University). We are especially indebted to Marian Branch of the RAND Publications Department for her exemplary editorial advice on the preparation of this document. We have also benefited from the comments and suggestions of various officials in the U.S. and ROK governments who reviewed the ongoing efforts of the research teams as well as draft versions of this report. Finally, we want to acknowledge the contribution of General Cho Sung Tae, formerly Assistant Minister for Policy at the ROK Ministry of National Defense and currently Commander, 2nd ROK Army, who first conceived of this project and urged the U.S. and ROK governments to undertake it.

ACRONYMS

ARF	ASEAN Regional Forum
ASEAN	Association of Southeast Asian Nations
CBMs	Confidence-building measures
CFC	Combined Forces Command
CONUS	Continental United States
DPRK	Democratic People's Republic of Korea (North Korea)
IAEA	International Atomic Energy Agency
KEDO	Korean Peninsula Energy Development Organization
NATO	North Atlantic Treaty Organization
OPCON	Operational Control
POMCUS	Prepositioned military equipment configured in unit sets
ROK	Republic of Korea
SLOCs	Sea lines of communication
USFK	U.S. Forces, Korea
WESTPAC	West Pacific (informal designation for U.S. forces deployed in the Western Pacific)
WHNS	Wartime host-nation support

Chapter One

WHY A NEW ALLIANCE?

PROFOUND CHANGES ARE POSSIBLE

Over the past 45 years, the United States and the Republic of Korea (ROK) have built a closely integrated political-military relationship through which both countries have helped ensure peace and stability on the peninsula and in Northeast Asia as a whole. Created in the aftermath of a highly destructive war launched against the South, a war that subsequently involved the United States and China as major combatants, the U.S.–ROK alliance encompassed a diverse set of mutual obligations and security commitments. The United States has since maintained a continuous military presence on the Korean peninsula. In addition, the United States and the ROK have devised numerous political, institutional, and operational arrangements so that the military establishments of both countries could collaborate fully in deterring renewed aggression and in defending the ROK should deterrence fail.

The maintenance of peace on the peninsula and South Korea's extraordinary record of economic and political accomplishments bear ample testimony to the contributions of U.S.–ROK security cooperation. The alliance has proven vital to achieving the security goals of both countries while also benefiting regional stability. In the aftermath of the Korean War, the Republic of Korea was a devastated country—vulnerable, acutely underdeveloped, and devoid of viable political institutions and processes. In the mid-1990s, the ROK has emerged as an industrial power of genuine consequence, a major actor in the world trading system, and a flourishing democratic state.

Equally important, South Korea's defense capabilities are increasingly robust, enabling the ROK to assume most of the responsibility for its own security while remaining firmly anchored to its alliance with the United States.

The strategic environment surrounding the Korean peninsula has also undergone profound change, especially over the past decade, and the changes have clearly benefited the interests of the ROK and the United States. The Soviet Union has ceased to exist, and with its demise the military competition between it and the United States as superpowers has also ended. China and Russia, rather than posing a direct threat to the security of the ROK and to U.S. forces deployed on the peninsula, enjoy full economic and political relations with South Korea. At the same time that North Korea has maintained its antagonistic stance toward the ROK, Northeast Asia as a whole has achieved prosperity and stability unimaginable several decades ago.

The U.S.–ROK alliance has adapted to these developments. Without such a response, the security ties between the United States and South Korea would have lost much of their relevance and vitality. To be sure, North Korean hostility toward the South remains undiminished: The forward deployment of the North's military forces, its active efforts to undermine the armistice arrangements, its ballistic missile program, and unresolved questions related to its nuclear weapons development continue to pose direct threats to the ROK and to U.S. forces on the peninsula. Given these considerations, the primary purpose of the alliance has remained intact: a combined strategy of deterrence and defense. But many of the alliance's dimensions and interrelationships are very different today from what they were 45 years ago. The Republic of Korea's growing prowess and self-assurance have enabled it to assume increased responsibility for its self-defense, permitting the United States to shift from a leading role to a supporting role in the alliance. Both countries have also sought to ensure that these changes not degrade Korea's security or America's capability to respond if a crisis occurs in the future.

But what of the future? Despite the continued confrontation and hostility between the two Koreas, many observers believe that significant change in the relationship between South and North is only a matter of time. Since the late 1980s, Chinese and Russian policies have undergone major shifts. Although Beijing and Moscow still seek to maintain the outward appearance of close ties with Pyongyang, both China and Russia have sharply diminished their political, economic, and security commitments to North Korea. At the same time, they have moved vigorously to build closer ties with the Republic of Korea. The region's economic and political dynamism finds Pyongyang increasingly isolated and falling even farther behind the ROK. Unless North Korea is prepared to adapt to the changes occurring all around it, its prospects appear increasingly bleak. Indeed, even if the North Korean leadership should seek a meaningful accommodation with the outside world (including the ROK), its longer-term political and economic viability would still be in doubt.

Thus, many observers believe that the process of change in the North is all but certain to lead to Korean unification—perhaps abruptly, as with German unification in October 1990. Even if the accommodation process does not induce such rapid change, any appreciable improvement in South-North relations could well presage a major reconfiguration in the regional security environment. If North Korea ceases to exist or if it no longer poses a major threat to peninsular security and stability, many of the security concerns that have dominated the U.S.–ROK alliance over the past four decades would no longer be relevant. (See Chapter Two.)

COLD WAR SECURITY ARRANGEMENTS MAY NO LONGER WORK

This study first seeks to establish the need for a changing alliance by addressing the viability of security arrangements devised and implemented during the Cold War. To numerous political and strategic analysts, the demise of the Soviet Union as a global political-military threat and the growing prosperity and stability of America's principal Cold War security partners invalidate the central propositions on which earlier security cooperation was built. Even though the incentives for sustaining close political relations between the United States and its Cold War allies seem self-evident, many assert that security cooperation need not be nearly as close in the future. With U.S. allies such as the ROK much more capable of ensuring their own security, many analysts argue that the need for a sustained U.S. forward presence will be much less in the years to come. Moreover, many observers believe that the interests of the United States and the

ROK will grow more divergent should the alliance's singular focus on the North Korean military threat cease. For example, increased economic competition, pressures for enhanced technological autonomy, or a significant shift in the major security preoccupations of either state could diminish the domestic support in both countries for maintaining a highly interactive and mutually supportive security relationship. Under such circumstances, the need for alliance integration would diminish appreciably, and the scale, size, and role of U.S. military forces in relation to Korea's future security needs would be sharply curtailed. (See Chapter Two.)

It would be imprudent to assume the inevitability of such policy developments, but it would be equally shortsighted to assume that present realities will persist indefinitely. If major change takes place on the peninsula, the United States and the Republic of Korea will need to reexamine the longer-term basis of their relationship and the value that each places on continued security cooperation. But the time to initiate such an examination is now—prior to any major reconfiguration of relations between South and North.

This study, the product of extensive deliberations and evaluations undertaken between RAND and the Korea Institute of Defense Analyses (KIDA), seeks to contribute to such a reexamination. In particular, it assesses the relevance of the U.S.–South Korean alliance in the context of transitions and transformations the alliance could face over the next decade. In this report, we focus primarily on the longer term rather than on the more near-term resource-allocation or program-level considerations that often dominate discussions and negotiations between alliance partners.

ALTERNATIVE SECURITY ARRANGEMENTS MUST BE IDENTIFIED

The principal objective of this study, therefore, was to identify and to evaluate a range of possibilities rather than to offer explicit predictions or to construct detailed scenarios. The two research teams sought to clarify the mutual benefits for the ROK and the United States in sustaining close security cooperation, and the potential implications for both countries should they fail to realize such a goal. Both research teams assumed that Northeast Asia will remain a region of ample and growing U.S. economic, political, and security interests.

In addition, the two teams recognized Korea's incentives to maintain close relations with the United States, even after peninsular unification. Both teams also assumed that major uncertainties and potential instabilities are likely to characterize peninsular and regional security over the coming decade. North Korea's political and economic viability, China's rapid economic advancement and its prospective emergence as a more fully developed major power, Russia's problematic transition to a market-oriented economy and democratic polity, and continued challenges to the maintenance of cohesion and cooperation among the market-oriented democracies constitute the most important of these factors. More than stating the obvious about the reality of these uncertainties, we need to acknowledge what we cannot project or predict with confidence. But by identifying a spectrum of possibilities and by assessing the potential implications of different conditions and circumstances, it is possible to discern policy choices that Korea and the United States could face in the years to come.

Such possibilities, however, depend fundamentally on the value that American and Korean policymakers attach to continued security cooperation. As we explore in greater detail in Chapter Two, the predominant focus of security planning during the Cold War was threat-based. The global rivalry between the United States and the Soviet Union and the simultaneous existence of a large, offensively oriented North Korean military threat furnished ready justifications for the alliance. The challenge of security collaboration in this transition period is to plan prudently in the face of existing security risks while seeking to induce North Korea to diminish the level of military confrontation with the ROK and to pursue accommodation and integration with the outside world.

THE ALTERNATIVES MUST THEN BE EVALUATED

If peninsular stability is realized in the longer term, the focus of U.S.–ROK security cooperation would need to shift toward regional concerns, and toward the building of multinational capabilities to address the needs of the post–Cold War international order. But continued security cooperation would depend on whether both countries believed that the U.S.–ROK alliance could be harnessed to different purposes and needs. Without an effort by both countries to impart a clearer sense of the intrinsic value that each state attaches to security cooperation, long-standing alliance bonds will weaken and support within both countries for close policy coordination will also diminish.

The future of the U.S.–ROK alliance and that of U.S. regional security strategy, therefore, require a careful assessment of alternative goals, policies, and security arrangements as both countries approach the twenty-first century. Without specifying the *what, why*, and *how* of future security cooperation, and without identifying the interests and policy objectives of the Republic of Korea and the United States under very different international conditions, the requirements for alliance renewal cannot be fully grasped. (See Chapter Three.)

To contribute to such understanding, RAND and KIDA explored and evaluated the security challenges both countries are likely to face, the conditions under which policy change is possible and appropriate, the adequacy of current security arrangements for addressing potential transitions, and the interests and capabilities of both states in pursuing security collaboration in the future. Through intensive discussion and comparison, the two teams reached a consensus on the desirability and feasibility of a continued U.S.–ROK alliance. Both teams concluded that the two countries would benefit far more by continuing security collaboration than by pursuing their interests through independent, uncoordinated national strategies. Because future alliance arrangements between the United States and its regional security partners will need to be different in design, scope, and in the apportionment of responsibility, an inability to develop new forms of security cooperation would prove disadvantageous to the interests of both the United States and the Republic of Korea.

To understand these potential challenges, RAND and KIDA deliberately sought to identify a broad range of possibilities, primarily to highlight how shifting environmental factors can alter the expectations and requirements of alliance partners, as well as influence the policy calculations of neighboring states. The balance of interests in an alliance—what states judge to be of primary value to their longer-term security, political, and economic goals and the price they are prepared to pay to achieve them—can shift markedly, and in un-anticipated ways.

The teams then gauged the relevance and appropriateness of different security concepts and arrangements, as perceived and understood by the two countries. By examining and appraising the issues that could confront the United States and Korea in the future, and by evaluating how continued security cooperation can help address these concerns, the research teams sought to identify common ground as well as areas of potential divergence. (See Chapter Four.)

DIFFERENT ALTERNATIVE PATHS MUST ALSO BE EXAMINED

Both teams also highlighted different paths that U.S.–ROK security cooperation could follow in the future. These alternative paths partly reflect the uncertainties that the two countries face in the peninsula and the region. But different paths and possibilities are also matters of policy design and emphasis. Depending on the end states that the two countries deem most beneficial to their respective long-term interests, the U.S.–ROK alliance could encompass new forms of cooperation or the countries could become far less interdependent in the future. But each possible path involves making conscious choices in national-level policy and trade-offs among various policy objectives. Our review and assessment of these alternative paths imparts a clearer sense of the care both countries must take in weighing their future alliance strategies. (See Chapter Five.)

BOTH THE UNITED STATES AND THE REPUBLIC OF KOREA MUST PREPARE ALTERNATIVE SECURITY ARRANGEMENTS

The need to plan for a very different future—even under conditions of continued North Korean threat—is incontestable. The events in Europe in the late 1980s and early 1990s offer a sobering reminder of the potential for rapid and unanticipated change. In Korea, it is impossible to know when major change—including unification—might occur. But should such change ensue, the peninsular and regional security environment would undergo a major transformation.

Several valid criticisms of our approach can be offered. A long-term planning study cannot anticipate or predict the actual circumstances that could confront policymakers, and models and concepts developed principally as research tools tend, unavoidably, to oversimplify. Many of the judgments and findings in this study do not fully capture the complexities of implementing change in day-to-day security operations, and they may not be sufficiently attuned to potential reactions from states elsewhere in the region. Finally, the evaluations of the two research teams may not accurately or fully depict the potential range of viewpoints that could emerge within both countries in the future.

ORGANIZATION OF THIS REPORT

RAND and KIDA pursued three broad research objectives:

- To identify and analyze the principal characteristics of and potential directions for long-term U.S.–ROK security cooperation

- To define a policy framework and criteria with which both countries could evaluate the suitability, feasibility, and consequences of alternative forms of security cooperation under shifting peninsular and regional conditions

- To highlight emerging policy issues that the study teams believe both governments will need to address in planning for the future.

This report addresses each objective in turn and summarizes the collective judgments that emerged from the deliberations of the two research teams.

In Chapter Two, we briefly review the origin and evolution of the alliance, and then discuss the peninsular and regional changes that are likely to redefine U.S.–ROK security cooperation over the coming decade.

In Chapter Three, we present four alternative models of future security cooperation, each reflecting a potential reconfiguration of the peninsular and regional security environment. In Chapter Four, we discuss the criteria identified and evaluated by the two research teams for determining the relevance and sustainability of the U.S.–ROK alliance under shifting security conditions. We also summarize the principal findings that emerged from this comparative evaluation. In Chapter Five, we specify four possible transition paths for future U.S.–ROK security cooperation and analyze the strengths and limitations of each path.

In Chapter Six, we examine some of the emerging policy challenges that the alliance seems likely to face in future years and identify considerations that both research teams believe warrant the attention of American and Korean decisionmakers.

RAND and KIDA believe that the civilian leaderships and military establishments of both countries need to undertake a joint assessment of their future policies and plans. Without initiating such a process, it will be impossible to arrive at a realistic consensus on longer-term policy goals and transitional measures that would advance the interests of both countries. The two research teams believe that this report helps identify some of the issues policymakers must begin to address.

Chapter Two

RETROSPECT AND PROSPECT

An alliance relationship encompasses a host of interrelated policy understandings and agreements. In fully developed form, it includes

- a strategic concept, or objective, that defines the shared obligations of alliance partners

- a common defense strategy through which roles, missions, and responsibilities are specified

- an agreement on the types and levels of forces required to implement a common defense strategy

- a range of more-specialized agreements on command relations, base arrangements, and burden-sharing.

In this chapter, we look at the dimensions that formed the initial U.S.–ROK alliance, then at changes taking place in these dimensions today and challenges for the future.

REVIEWING THE HISTORICAL RECORD

Security cooperation between the United States and the Republic of Korea first developed under circumstances that bear little resemblance to those of today. Six months after having excluded Korea from the U.S. security perimeter in Asia in early 1950, the United States deemed the defeat of North Korean aggression vital to America's global strategic interests. Yet it was not a sudden recognition of Korea's intrinsic economic or political importance that impelled the United States to act, especially in view of the South's very low level of development. Rather, the Korean peninsula had abruptly emerged as the locale over which vital U.S. strategic interests had become engaged. The North's attack on the South manifested three principal threats to U.S. vital interests: It portended the rise of a hostile coalition of states led by a power threatening hegemony over the entire Asian mainland; it reflected the challenge of an ideology antithetical to American values; and it raised the possibility of the denial of U.S. economic access to East Asia as a whole. Although American strategists had previously voiced concern about these threats, the North Korean attack made these threats matters of utmost urgency for the U.S. position in the Western Pacific.

The U.S. intervention in Korea underscored three primary strategic objectives that have since remained central to U.S. policy in Asia and the Pacific: (1) to prevent the domination of Northeast Asia by a hostile power or coalition of states; (2) to foster an environment in which practices and institutions supportive of U.S. values and interests could take root; and (3) to ensure that markets and resources remained accessible to U.S. economic involvement and development. The containment of communist power, the defeat of North Korea's attack on the South, the deterrence of renewed aggression by North Korea, and the stabilization of the U.S. position throughout the region were all corollaries to these larger strategic objectives. Although these interests and objectives have been modified in subsequent decades, they still remain defining elements in U.S. policy.

The ROK's vital strategic interests (especially in the early decades of the alliance) were highly circumscribed, reflecting its low level of economic development and its lack of workable institutions. Its preeminent concerns were to achieve political viability, to uphold national sovereignty and national security, and to foster conditions that would contribute to longer-term economic development. These interests presupposed an ability (in cooperation with the United States) to defeat renewed aggression from the North, to realize national reconstruction and development, and to achieve internal stability. Premised on an immediate military threat to a highly vulnerable South Korean state, the U.S.–ROK alliance was one among a number of defense relationships forged by the United States along the Asian rimland in the 1950s. South Korea's security and well-being were closely tied to American concerns with the stability and viability of other regional actors, Japan in particular.

The accomplishments of the alliance over its 45-year history have been incontestable. First and foremost, deterrence has been maintained, although (given the magnitude of North Korea's military capabilities arrayed against the South) it has entailed large, ongoing combined efforts by the United States and the ROK to ensure the peace. Second, South Korea has experienced extraordinary economic growth, transforming itself from an underdeveloped, predominantly agrarian economy to a robust industrial and leading export power in only a quarter century. Third, the ROK now enjoys a political emergence on the international scene that parallels its economic development. Domestically, this has led to the creation and maturation of democratic political institutions and processes. Internationally, the Republic of Korea has achieved near-universal diplomatic recognition; normal relations with Russia and China and full entry into the United Nations are among the most recent and most significant evidence of that recognition. Fourth, South Korean forces have assumed a progressively greater share of the responsibility for the country's defense, permitting the United States to concentrate its security role in those areas where North Korean weapon deployments and military strategy still pose a particular risk to ROK security. Fifth, all these trends have proven conducive to enhancing stability and democracy within South Korean society, and to facilitating stability throughout Northeast Asia.

These developments have made the ROK a much more important partner of the United States, with the relationship far less unbalanced than in the past. The ROK has continued to rely on its alliance with the United States, but the relationship is far more equitable and less dependent. Indeed, there is an explicit connection between separate but complementary goals: the U.S. desire that its regional allies fulfill an increased share of the responsibility for their self-defense and the ROK desire to enhance its autonomy and responsibility for securing its own long-term interests.

But pursuit of common interests could prove more difficult to achieve in the future. The Republic of Korea is increasingly coming of age, and it expects more of a say in the alliance's future direction. At the same time, the United States is adapting to a more diversified set of post–Cold War policy challenges that could redefine its activities and policy emphases. Some potential divergences are evident in the separate efforts by RAND and KIDA to specify the security interests of the two countries, as outlined in Figures 2.1 and 2.2. These estimates highlight a substantial convergence. However, the common interests are dominated by military considerations—factors manifested most fully in a high-threat environment. Under less-threatening circumstances, the focus of policymakers shifts to a broader set of concerns.

Thus, the focus on a direct security threat draws allies together, but the reduction or elimination of a threat results in movement away from the immediate military requirements of an alliance. A state less preoccupied with an active military threat will devote increased attention to other, long-term national priorities—for example, material well-being for its citizens, economic advantage, technological advancement and autonomy (including in national defense), and diminished expenditures and commitments to national security.

The incentives for accommodating the interests of an ally can also diminish in the context of altered national priorities. Although shared values and broader common interests are likely to check some areas of potential divergence, an ally could shift toward more-exclusive definitions of *national interest*. Thus, if the United States and the ROK are to avoid a narrow focus on their own self-interest, they must consciously seek to identify and articulate a broader set of mutual interests on which the well-being and security of both countries depend: Doing so without weakening their political and security bonds is the major challenge the two countries are likely to face in the coming decade.

EMERGING CHALLENGES

Although both American and Korean policy calculations have shifted markedly in the aftermath of the dissolution of the Soviet Union, the effects on U.S. global strategy have been especially pronounced. The United States no longer faces a challenger state seeking to contest U.S. interests on a worldwide basis; consequently, Korea does not serve as the focal point in global strategic competition that it did in the past. But the uncertainties in Northeast Asia remain substantial and provide the United States and the ROK with clear incentives to sustain close political, economic, and security ties. The peninsula remains divided, with highly antagonistic relations between South

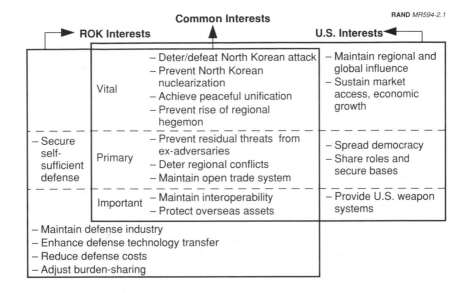

Figure 2.1—Security Interests of the United States and the Republic of Korea: KIDA's Perspective

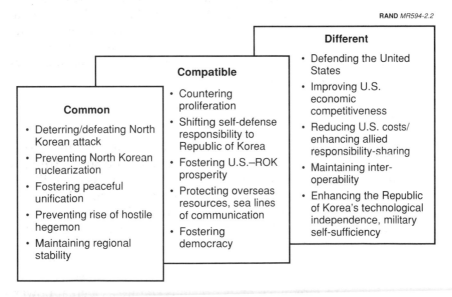

Figure 2.2—RAND's Assessment of U.S.–ROK Security Interests and Objectives

and North. North Korea still maintains major offensive military deployments against South Korea, and it is still not reconciled to the reality of the ROK's power and international legitimacy. These considerations lend immediacy and major import to future developments on the peninsula, including the continued danger of a highly destructive military conflict. In addition, the Korean peninsula is the only locale in the world where the security interests of four major powers—the United States, Russia, China, and Japan—intersect.

This larger regional context is the major factor affecting the longer-term interests of both countries. East Asia's rapid economic, technological, and military development portends a major change in the global balance of power, but this change finds the broader political and strategic patterns in the region highly unsettled. Despite the region's extraordinary dynamism and increasing economic integration, a comprehensive political and security structure is lacking, which injects substantial uncertainty into the framework of great-power relations. Bilateral security ties between the United States and the ROK and between the United States and Japan aside, no institutionalized security structure exists in Northeast Asia to restrain potential geopolitical rivalries among the United States, China, Russia, and Japan. Consultative arrangements (with the exception of bilateral security ties) are episodic and *ad hoc*. In addition, developments in each of the region's major powers underlie the sense of uncertainty in the region as a whole.

Russia

Russia's greatly diminished political and military fortunes are among the principal elements of regional uncertainty. The Soviet Union's disintegration and the attendant weakening of Russia's military power and presence in East Asia have greatly reduced Moscow's stature, capabilities, and regional influence. Although Russia still maintains substantial military forces in the region, this military role seems increasingly subsidiary in Moscow's policy calculations, especially in the context of Russia's pervasive domestic preoccupations and far larger concerns with instability to its south and west. Russia still aspires to restore much of its previous stature as a great power, but Moscow's capacity to shape events in areas of historical Russian influence, including the Korean peninsula, has been greatly reduced.

Even as Russia has appreciably expanded its political and economic links with the ROK, the prospects for its full integration in the region are highly unsettled by Russian politics and foreign policy. Although Russia no longer assumes a militarily destabilizing role on the peninsula, the states of East Asia—including the ROK—must heed the lack of a clearly defined Russian geopolitical role within the region, Russia's rapidly degrading power, and the widespread upheaval in its internal affairs as providing the potential for instability in East Asia.

China

The waning of Russia's regional influence has coincided with the rise of Chinese power and China's increasing strategic weight in East Asia. China has achieved sustained economic growth for a decade and a half. It is now a major force in regional trade relations (including those with the ROK), as well as a major trading partner of the United States. Its growing economic power has been matched by increased political influence and heightened attention to modernizing its military forces. In addition, China has long viewed its vital interests as engaged along its northeastern borders. China also remains North Korea's most important political and security partner and its principal source of economic support, though at much diminished levels. But Korean unification would cause the regional security environment to be reconfigured drastically and would immediately affect China's vital national security interests.

Quite apart from the prospect of Korean unification, China maintains ambitions to emerge as a true major power, which will entail the development of more-capable Chinese military forces in the twenty-first century—forces that are commensurate with its rapid political and economic development. For the first time in its modern history, China would abut a strong, unified Korean state. Even before the peninsula's reunification, China is predicating its longer-term interests on a much more comprehensive economic and political relationship with the Republic of Korea. But a unified Korea will define the new power realities in Northeast Asia in dramatically different terms.

At the same time, China's strategic objectives and power potential are being watched closely by all regional states. China clearly aspires to a central position in the future regional order, but its readiness to achieve this position through cooperation and effective consultation with its neighbors remains uncertain. This situation finds China's neighbors respectful yet concerned about the implications of its emergence as a genuine major power.

China's longer-term relations with the United States and Japan also remain uncertain and subject to repeated stresses and strains. And even as the Chinese aspire to more-collaborative relations with other regional states, they also continue to acknowledge conflicting territorial claims with a number of their neighbors. Both the United States and the ROK are endeavoring to build stable, mutually beneficial relations with China, but the latter's size, dynamism, and military potential are inescapable.

The Chinese are also in the midst of a profound internal transition. New generations of leaders increasingly dominate the country's politics, and they are grappling with the prodigious challenges of maintaining political and social stability while moving the country toward a market-based economy.

It is against these realities that all of China's neighbors must prudently plan for the longer term.

Japan

Japan's future political-strategic role also assumes crucial significance in the region's future. Although still integrally tied to its alliance with the United States, Japan is now deliberating its longer-term options and strategies, a process of debate that is closely linked to Japan's continuing internal political realignment: Contending political forces hope to achieve a new equilibrium to supplant the long-dominant pattern of one-party rule. As part of this process, policymakers in Tokyo hope to realize a new consensus about the country's longer-term policy goals and directions. Although there is still strong support for sustaining the U.S. alliance, other voices are calling for a shift toward a more "Asia-based" foreign policy. But any such policy reorientation also raises major concerns among Japan's neighbors, including Korea, given Japan's former colonial rule in Korea and its role throughout East Asia during the Pacific War.

As with China, the unification of the peninsula means that Japan will no longer face a weak and divided Korea. The ROK's ability to achieve a more amicable long-term relationship with Japan will depend on the efforts of both Japan and the ROK, each of which simultaneously hopes to maintain close relations with the United States. However, the states of the region are now highly developed and far less vulnerable, creating possibilities for both cooperation and rivalry at the same time—far different from the Cold War period.

Need for New Institutional Arrangements

The United States and the states of the region thus face a major challenge in devising new norms that more fully reflect the emerging regional realities while addressing concerns left over from the past. There is a need to develop institutional arrangements to supplant the Cold War structures and to integrate the emerging economies and polities of the region in a manner commensurate with their increased capabilities and growing self-confidence.

The development of the ASEAN Regional Forum (ARF) and calls for a multilateral security dialogue in Northeast Asia reflect the incipient challenges of the post–Cold War regional security environment. A principal goal of the process of institutional change is to help ensure sustained economic and political cooperation between the United States and the region. A new framework must also help manage lingering disputes in post–Cold War Asia while avoiding a situation in which states seek unilateral political, economic, or security advantage. Excessive nationalization of security policies would reflect a collective failure to capitalize on opportunities for enhanced integration and collaboration, thereby seriously detracting from a general pattern of growing stability and prosperity.

East Asia's Economic Transformation

East Asia's economic transformation is also pivotal in any assessment of the region's future. South Korea is among the newly industrializing states that have elevated the Asia-Pacific region to an area of paramount American interest. Over the past three decades, the economic growth and technological development of the region as a whole have consistently outpaced those of every other area of the world, steadily expanding the region's contributions to global economic output and to world trade. According to recent estimates, the Asia-Pacific region's share of total world income will increase from approximately 25 percent in the early 1990s to more than 33 percent by the early years of the next century.

U.S. trade with the Asia-Pacific region makes up a growing share of total U.S. trade. According to recent estimates, the region's share of total U.S. trade in 1993 was 35.2 percent, nearly double that of Western Europe (22.2 percent). Projections to the early twenty-first century indicate that this pattern will become even more pronounced: Asia-Pacific trade with the United States will more than double that of Western Europe, 37.6 percent as opposed to 18.5 percent (Marcus Noland, *Implications of Asian Economic Growth*, New York: Council on Foreign Relations, Asia Project Working Paper, November 1994, Table 3). Although U.S. foreign direct investment in Asia and the Pacific still lags well behind that in Europe (17 percent as opposed to 49 percent, according to 1993 data), the trends in the early 1990s are also pronounced, with major increases in U.S. investment both in the region and with individual countries. This pattern seems virtually certain to persist or to accelerate further over the coming decade (Mark Mason, *Foreign Direct Investment in East Asia: Trends and Critical U.S. Policy Issues*, New York: Council on Foreign Relations, Asia Project Working Paper, November 1994, Table 1 and Figure 1).

Although the ROK's economy is dwarfed in size by those of China and Japan, the country's location and continued economic dynamism place it at the center of this remarkable shift in global economic power. Even if the rate of Asian economic growth (including that of the ROK) should slow somewhat over the coming decade, the region's economic and technological enhancement will remain critical for the global economy and for the United States' future economic well-being.

Potential for Military Conflict

The end of the U.S.–Soviet global strategic rivalry, East Asia's incomplete and highly uncertain transition to a post–Cold War security order, and the region's ever-increasing centrality to the global economy define the principal domains in which U.S. regional strategy will operate for the indefinite future. Korea remains central to all three domains. The continued high level of military confrontation on the peninsula underscores the potential for major armed conflict. Renewed warfare in Korea or a disorderly reunification process would prove highly destabilizing and damaging for the Korean people, but its political, economic, and security consequences would go well beyond the peninsula. A major military conflict would directly involve American forces and would also affect the interests and security calculations of other major powers. These considerations lend immediacy to U.S. and ROK deliberations over their future security ties and defense strategies.

SUMMARY

An understanding of the question of what form the U.S.–ROK security alliance should take in the future must begin with identification of the common goals and interests that continue to animate the bilateral alliance. In the estimation of the two research teams, the following goals and interests are a complementary set of *vital* interests that are still relevant in the post–Cold War era: (1) deterring North Korean attack and defeating North Korea should deterrence fail; (2) realizing a peninsula free of nuclear weapons; (3) fostering the peaceful and democratic unification of the peninsula; and (4) ensuring maintenance of a stable balance of power in Asia and the Pacific. The future of the peninsula remains a dominant security preoccupation of both countries; the reality of continued threats to peace and stability on the peninsula cannot be ignored.

However, even as both countries confront present dangers, they must also begin to think about the longer term. The political, economic, and strategic role of a unified Korea will be a central factor in the future political and strategic patterns of East Asia. This Korea would clearly aspire to a stature in the region commensurate with the economic, political, and military weight of such a powerful and important state.

But what would a unified Korea imply for the future of the region and for the U.S. position in East Asia? How might Korea seek to fulfill its aspirations in relation to Japan, Russia, and China? How would Korea's longer-term goals and interests converge with or diverge from America's future regional and global policies? In essence, how might the ROK and the United States judge the possibilities for continued collaboration once the common security threat that drew them together for decades ceased to exist? To explore these complex issues, we need to turn our attention to the options available to the ROK and the United States for sustaining their security collaboration in the future.

Chapter Three

IDENTIFYING SECURITY ALTERNATIVES
FOR THE FUTURE

Despite the growing interest in the strategic implications of a unified Korea, the U.S.–ROK security relationship is still shaped first and foremost by prevailing political and security conditions on the peninsula. The current security relationship has been in place for so long that it is sometimes difficult to imagine circumstances under which major change might occur. This study does not explore North Korea's future prospects and policy options in any detail, although this topic warrants careful examination by the United States and the ROK, especially given the leadership transition in the North and North Korea's highly uncertain political and economic prospects.

The principal analytic challenge faced by the two research teams was to assess the value and relevance of different forms of security cooperation under changing peninsular conditions according to different criteria of effectiveness, and the political and military circumstances that would make various security alternatives especially relevant. Both teams were mindful of the existing military threats posed by North Korea, as well as of the continued absence of a verified history of the North Korean nuclear weapons program. North Korean military capabilities and operational readiness have both degraded in recent years, but the forward deployment of Pyongyang's military forces and its potent weapons inventory would still enable North Korea to inflict significant losses on ROK and U.S. forces in a military conflict, even though the ultimate outcome of such a conflict is not in doubt.

Given these circumstances, both research teams recognized the need to be prudent in evaluating the dangers and risks on the peninsula, and in assessing alternative courses of action in future U.S.–ROK alliance relations. For analytic purposes, however, it was necessary to consider how changes in the peninsular security setting might affect future alliance strategies and defense requirements.

In this chapter, we summarize the efforts of RAND and KIDA to identify potential security alternatives in future U.S.–ROK relations. The two teams focused on three principal questions in defining those alternatives:

- What are the discernible models of security cooperation between the United States and Korea, at present and in the future?

- What are the principal characteristics of collaboration—specific strategic concepts and operational dimensions—under each alternative?

- Under what circumstances—transitional events—would each alternative be most relevant to the two countries?

Deliberations between alliance partners frequently focus on force levels, operational military concepts, and programmatic activities. But it is imperative to first identify the broader strategic concerns that provide structure and logic to the more narrowly defined elements of security cooperation. Thus, the assessments of the two research teams focused on the major policy alternatives, the political-military conditions associated with them, and possible indicators of change in the security environment. Understanding each consideration is integral to evaluating the relevance of different strategic concepts under a range of potential future conditions.

After extensive discussion, RAND and KIDA focused on four principal security alternatives in the U.S.–ROK alliance: (1) a robust peninsular alliance, (2) a reconfigured peninsular alliance, (3) a regional security alliance, and (4) a political alliance. The alternatives are presented in "ideal-type" form and should not be seen as formal models or policy proposals. In line with the above three questions, for each alternative we provide different estimates of:

- the peninsular security situation

- the primary focus of security cooperation between the two countries

- the obligations and responsibilities of each country under the posited political and security conditions.

By specifying these alternatives and highlighting how different levels of integration and collaboration would affect the choices available to policymakers, we can better understand the interaction of planning and policy, both now and in the future.

ALTERNATIVE ONE: A ROBUST PENINSULAR ALLIANCE

Peninsular Security Situation

The first security alternative embodies the existing approach to the U.S.–ROK alliance, which posits a fully integrated military alliance for deterring any attack on the ROK and defending the ROK should deterrence fail. It emphasizes maintaining a stalwart forward defense so long as the North Korean threat persists. Moreover, such a concept does not preclude augmentation of U.S.–ROK combined defense capabilities if adverse security developments (for example, enhanced North Korean unconventional warfare capabilities) require increased attention. But the essential strategic concept remains that of a close military alliance focused principally on defense of the ROK's borders against perceived threats.

From this concept, it is possible to apportion American and ROK security responsibilities according to the current capabilities of the two military establishments. The ROK has been able to fulfill an increasing range of responsibilities as its military capabilities and operational experiences have been further enhanced, especially over the past decade. During that time, both countries have consciously sought to increase the ROK's military self-sufficiency and encourage command autonomy, and to gradually reduce the U.S. military presence as these twin goals are more fully realized. The December 1994 return of armistice operational control of select ROK units to the ROK government is the most recent and most tangible dimension of these policy changes.

Shifts in U.S.–ROK defense cooperation are taking place within a well-understood, mutually agreed series of steps that in no way invalidate the underlying logic of a continued peninsular security alliance. Appreciable U.S. forces remain in place on the peninsula, and (in conjunction with continental United States [CONUS]-based forces) they remain integral to realizing the goal of a combined defense strategy.

Security Cooperation

Highly integrated security cooperation remains undisturbed between the Republic of Korea and the United States under these circumstances. As long as North Korean forces represent an appreciable offensive military threat deployed against the ROK, a robust peninsular alliance remains relevant and provides the principal context for security deliberations between the two countries. Since the precise configuration of U.S. forces remains dependent on the military threat to the ROK, U.S. military capabilities could be enhanced if circumstances warrant. The augmentation of U.S. forces during spring 1994, when tensions over the status of the North Korean nuclear weapons program increased sharply, demonstrates the capacity of both countries to reinforce deterrence during a period of heightened tensions. It also highlights that any shifts in policy or in the U.S.–ROK combined defense strategy should continue to depend on specific conditions on the peninsula, rather than be mandated by a timetable or schedule.

Although a peninsular strategic concept has been pursued over the past four decades, its logic would not be automatically invalidated should the North Korean threat be eliminated and reunification take place. A unified Korean state would still face the challenge of ensuring its security and protecting its borders, which would then abut China and Russia. The character of Korea's defense strategy and needs would also depend on Korea's political relations with Japan, and on the status of the U.S.–Japan relationship. Thus, U.S.–Korean security cooperation in the post-unification era would be shaped by U.S. security requirements and interests in a redefined regional setting. Even today, U.S. forces are deployed in Northeast Asia for reasons unrelated to the North Korean threat (for example, contingencies in the Persian Gulf and helping to maintain a satisfactory balance of power in the region). However, U.S. military assets necessary to the defense of the ROK need not be deployed in-country under all circumstances, especially if alternative options (for example, reliance on carrier-based air assets) are deemed preferable.

Obligations of Each Country

Under existing conditions, the United States and the ROK each fulfill important functions needed to ensure the combined defense of the Republic of Korea. In addition to providing ground and air forces for the initial forward defense of the southern half of the peninsula, American forces continue to perform specialized roles and responsibilities (for example, intelligence and early warning), and also retain principal responsibility for maritime security and outside reinforcement in the event of major hostilities. ROK forces assume a primary responsibility for ground combat under this security alternative; a secondary ROK role is to support U.S. air and naval missions and to provide wartime host-nation support (WHNS) to U.S. forces deployed to Korea.

Although the United States and Korea would need to jointly determine security arrangements appropriate to the post-unification era, under less-threatening conditions the level of integration in U.S.–Korean defense planning would almost certainly diminish. Depending on the larger security environment and Korea's degree of self-sufficiency, U.S. forces might remain to provide highly specialized support for air defense and for command, control, communications, and intelligence. It is possible that a ground combat brigade might also remain, but this requirement might also be met by periodic rotation of Marine and Army units deployed elsewhere in the Pacific. The future U.S. manpower levels and force requirements would depend on judgments about the perceived need for continued U.S. forces, potential alternatives to in-country deployments, and deficiencies in Korea's defense capabilities.

ALTERNATIVE TWO: A RECONFIGURED PENINSULAR ALLIANCE

Peninsular Security Situation

The second security alternative posits continued attention to peninsular defense under a still-divided Korea, but with responsibility entrusted far more fully to ROK forces. The U.S.–ROK alliance would continue to operate in a highly coordinated fashion, but the United States would focus principally on a reinforcement role. The prevailing strategic concept would be of an alliance primarily for force reconstitution (i.e., remobilizing U.S. capabilities) and crisis management. Because of the diminished contribution of U.S. forces, force levels on the peninsula and the mix of U.S. capabilities deployed in Korea would be adjusted significantly. U.S. forces on the peninsula would provide the infrastructure necessary for ensuring rapid reinforcement in a crisis. There would also very likely be periodic additional deployments for combined exercises, because the two countries would want to ensure no weakening of deterrence and defense arrangements. As with the robust peninsular concept (Alternative One), U.S. forces in Korea could also be part of a larger strategy to reassure regional states of the U.S. commitment to maintaining the Northeast Asian balance of power, especially should fluidity and uncertainty in great-power relations persist.

The prevailing security circumstances under this alternative would be different from those posited under a robust peninsular alliance. Several factors would attest to such change. The North Korean threat would have diminished appreciably, and political tension between South and North would have abated. At the same time, ROK force enhancements would have progressed to the point where the need for a significant in-country presence of U.S. forces would have decreased. In essence, the Republic of Korea would have moved much closer to the strategic goal of military autonomy posited under the first security alternative, with North Korean forces no longer deemed nearly as great a military threat.

Under these circumstances, the peninsular military balance would be far more stable and secure, realized, preferably, through verified, asymmetric reductions in North Korean forces. Related measures to diminish or altogether eliminate North Korea's capability for offensive warfare against the South would be a corollary to such steps. At the same time, the existence of a North Korean nuclear weapons program would have to be determined conclusively and eliminated, and the South-North denuclearization agreement would have to be implemented and the South-North accommodation process activated fully. Such developments would attest to a major alteration in peninsular security circumstances, thereby permitting a reconfiguration of U.S.–ROK alliance arrangements. But uncertainties in the larger regional environment might well dictate that an appreciable U.S. military presence be maintained, irrespective of the degree of North Korean threat.

Security Cooperation

Under the second alternative, the Republic of Korea would assume the preponderance of responsibility for shaping its defense strategy, force posture, and command system for an initial defense of its borders. The ROK would be expected to meet most threats on its own, without appreciable reliance on external assistance. The ROK would turn to the United States only if a major crisis threatened to overwhelm its capacity for self-defense. The United States, though still serving as the major political partner of the ROK, would have principally an offshore military presence, continuing to provide a nuclear umbrella under existing security arrangements and joining with West Pacific (WESTPAC) and CONUS-based reinforcements in a major crisis.

Obligations of Each Country

Under such conditions, the United States would need to maintain sufficient communications and intelligence assets and appropriate logistics support to guarantee effective and prompt utilization of needed equipment in a crisis. Such support would extend to maintaining wartime reserve stocks and prepositioned military equipment configured in unit sets (POMCUS). Smaller ground, air, and naval contingents would remain in Korea to facilitate peacetime training and development of common doctrine and operational procedures. But most training would be undertaken by periodic deployment of U.S. forces for combined exercises, and U.S. manpower levels would be appreciably lower than those maintained under Alternative One.

ALTERNATIVE THREE: A REGIONAL SECURITY ALLIANCE

Peninsular Security Situation

A third policy alternative posits a major shift in the direction and emphasis of U.S.–ROK security collaboration. The strategic concept of peninsular defense might remain in place, but it would be augmented by an emphasis on roles and responsibilities beyond the peninsula, either conducted between the ROK and the United States or in collaboration with the United States and other U.S. allies and security partners. How strongly the latter concept would be emphasized would depend on peninsular defense requirements, but the emphasis in strategy and planning would shift to roles and responsibilities elsewhere in Northeast Asia (for example, maritime security). Building on a secure Korean peninsula as its geopolitical foundation, a transformed U.S.–ROK relationship would focus primarily on projecting security and stability outward: elsewhere in Northeast Asia and, to the extent appropriate, into more-distant locales in the Asia-Pacific region.

Security Cooperation

The degree of collaboration on regional missions would depend heavily on conditions on the Korean peninsula. Should a major North Korean threat persist, any missions beyond the peninsula would necessarily remain quite modest. As the North Korean threat abated, the U.S.–ROK alliance would become more flexible— especially in a post-unification context, assuming no other threat emerged to endanger Korean security. However, even if a regional security arrangement were to develop, it would likely postulate that a strong bilateral security relationship be maintained.

Regional security collaboration could offer at least three possible approaches, with the precise force mix and structure varying according to the postulated strategic concept and its operational requirements:

A CONUS-Centered Regional Alliance. U.S. forces would be deployed predominantly from U.S. territory, and America's regional deployments would be limited to specialized functions. This approach would require close collaboration with regional partners, and the United States would seek to maximize the application of new technologies in a power-projection role.

A Distributed Regional Alliance. In this approach, both the United States and the ROK would pursue regional roles, linked directly to U.S. forces deployed in Korea and elsewhere in Asia and the Pacific. The primary focus of U.S. regional defense planning would be to make U.S. forces in the region as complementary as possible to those of the ROK and other regional partners, thus minimizing redundancies and inefficiencies through enhanced cooperation.

A Peninsula-Centered Regional Alliance. In this approach, the United States (in combination with ROK forces) would deploy dedicated forces on the peninsula sufficient to respond to particular regional security requirements, independent of arrangements with other U.S. allies in the region.

Obligations of Each Country

The contributions the ROK would make and the obligations it would assume would depend on the precise type of regional security structure. At a minimum, the ROK would be expected to maintain forces dedicated to specific regional missions. The ROK would also provide bases and access for U.S. forces in their regional role; ROK forces would participate in regional peacekeeping operations, including joint and combined exercises; and the ROK could expect to explore multilateral security linkages with other countries in the region.

A central feature of this security alternative would be combined training and operation of U.S. and ROK forces for security responsibilities beyond the peninsula. Such activities might initially be concentrated in Northeast Asia, but they could ultimately extend to other locales. Future collaboration would therefore likely be most pronounced with respect to U.S. and ROK air and naval forces, but combined ground force operations might also be pursued for peacekeeping and crisis-management capabilities. Thus, the ROK would need to set aside military forces for designated responsibilities apart from peninsular defense. For example, such forces might help constitute the building blocks of a multinational rapid-reaction force consisting of ground, air, naval, and mobility assets. Creation of any such force would require both that an integrated command structure be developed for power projection and regional security and that significant combined training operations be conducted to ensure interoperability in doctrine and procedures for missions beyond Korea's borders. Burden-sharing arrangements would be determined almost exclusively by the respective commitments to such a multinational force, and roles and responsibilities would be allocated to ensure complementarity and to maximize functional specialization of forces.

Under this security alternative, a significant U.S. military presence would likely remain in Korea, but it would be primarily for regional security rather than for peninsular defense. Thus, the mix of U.S. forces deployed on the peninsula would be virtually certain to undergo appreciable change, including reduction or complete withdrawal of U.S. ground forces and an increase in U.S. power-projection capabilities being deployed on the peninsula. American forces would be based at locations that allowed for needed training and for efficient deployment outside Korea. Access to airlift facilities and seaports would be crucial for the U.S. presence. The total size and distributions of U.S. capabilities would be driven by the designated mission, the requirements for regional power projection, the extent of combined training with ROK and other allied forces, and the degree of U.S. obligations to a multinational force. In design, direction, and purpose, a regional alliance concept would depart markedly from present policies.

ALTERNATIVE FOUR: A POLITICAL ALLIANCE

Peninsular Security Situation

The final security alternative represents the outer limits of dismantling the present alliance structure. It envisions an ROK sufficiently confident about its self-defense capability that it would no longer perceive an appreciable security relationship with the United States as being necessary. The guiding strategic concept would be purely political, with no supporting military superstructure.

Security Cooperation

This alternative would be similar in concept and design to NATO in 1949 (that is, prior to the creation of an integrated command structure). U.S.–ROK security interactions would focus primarily on high-level political and security consultations; extensive military coordination and peacetime combined defense planning would virtually cease. There would also be little or no effort to coordinate regional security policies between the two countries. The ROK would assume full responsibility for its own defense and would design its strategy and force posture without binding U.S. assurances of outside reinforcement in a crisis.

U.S. military forces could be available as potential reinforcements in an emergency, but no explicit commitments would be made in advance, and no specific programmatic steps would be undertaken to ensure the capability for rapid reinforcement. The United States would thus become a purely over-the-horizon military power with respect to Korea: It would be committed to ROK security in political but not military terms, and any wartime contributions would be determined only at the time of actual events, not arranged in advance.

Obligations of Each Country

The U.S. military presence in Korea would be token in size and commitment, reflecting this highly truncated concept. Small units might remain to perform liaison, security assistance, logistics, and communications and intelligence functions. If reception facilities were maintained, they would be largely dormant rather than fully operational. A token commitment of U.S. airpower (for example, a fighter squadron or an air defense battery) might remain, but nearly all combat units would be withdrawn, and ground combat units would depart fully. A program of exercises might continue, but on a small scale, not oriented toward a major reinforcement by the United States. This security alternative would be an alliance in name only.

COMPARING THE SECURITY ALTERNATIVES

These four policy alternatives comprise a broad range of possibilities for the future of the U.S.–ROK security relationship. In differentiating among the four approaches, we recommend not overemphasizing their differences as much as viewing the actual practice of any form of security cooperation as a continuum of needs, objectives, and procedures. This said, each model (by maximizing particular policy preferences) "translates" into different results and consequences for bilateral and regional relations. For example, a robust peninsular alliance is the most fully integrated of security relationships. To varying degrees, the other three security approaches would enable the United States and the ROK to retain initiative outside the confines of the alliance while needing to weigh those "positive" aspects against the risks and uncertainties that less-binding security ties could entail.

Our purpose here is not to posit an optimal or preferred model for future security collaboration, however. Judgments about policy preferences, in the final analysis, reflect the goals that states want to maximize, the conditions under which a particular policy alternative is expected to operate, and the uncertainties and risks that leaders are seeking to manage. Conversely, opting for a security alternative that maximizes certainty and predictability could prove very costly politically or budgetarily. It might also prove overly rigid in the context of larger shifts in the regional environment and insufficiently adaptive in relation to abrupt or unanticipated change.

Thus, weighing policy alternatives is a process that represents a complex interaction of competing policy objectives, not in the abstract but in the face of substantial uncertainties about the future and in relation to the interests that countries are seeking to maximize. The relevance and potential limitations of these relationships become clear only by such evaluation.

To gauge the four security alternatives more fully, we need to assess how they might function across a range of futures, and in the context of different policy needs that the United States and the ROK could confront in the coming decade.

Chapter Four

EVALUATING THE SECURITY ALTERNATIVES

The United States and the Republic of Korea hope to build upon past successes in alliance policy. But the uncertainties and challenges of the future will very likely require that the relationship move beyond the peninsular logic that has defined these two countries' security ties over the past four decades. In addition, under conditions of diminished military threat, security cooperation would encompass a broader range of national goals less focused on warfighting requirements. Both countries, therefore, need to prepare for conditions that their past experience as allies does not fully enable them to address or anticipate.

This uncertainty renders the evaluation of future alliance concepts especially difficult. Rather than offer detailed scenarios for the coming decade, the two teams sought to focus on a range of plausible conditions and on a more focused set of factors likely to shape future U.S. and ROK policy calculations. This approach enabled RAND and KIDA to specify an array of possible conditions, then to assess what demands those conditions might impose on both states. The two research teams devised organizing concepts around which specific policy alternatives could be subjected to more-detailed evaluation. Two steps proved especially crucial: (1) identifying the operative political and security circumstances on the peninsula, in this chapter designated by a *phase* most conducive to a particular security concept, or alternative, defined in Chapter Three, and (2) specifying criteria for measuring the appropriateness of those alternative security concepts to the interests and strategies of both countries. After extensive deliberations, the research teams agreed upon the phases and criteria, which are the subject of this chapter.

POSSIBLE PENINSULAR PHASES

In reviewing prospective conditions on the Korean peninsula, three "states of the world" seemed logical and plausible; each directly determines the prevailing security circumstances. In identifying these alternative states, we have not sought to predict or estimate when the transition from one condition to another might take place. The transition process could prove uneven, inconclusive, and subject to reversal. Indeed, a central conclusion of this study is that alliance strategies cannot be formulated according to a timetable or schedule; the precise conditions and needs of both the United States and the ROK must serve as the decisive factors in policy evaluation. But the different states, or phases, could be triggered by particular events, even if we cannot specify with certainty when such events might transpire. The objective of this portion of the analyses is to specify the defining characteristics of a given *phase*—that is, the outcomes that would need to transpire before policymakers could conclude that a different peninsular phase had arrived, in whole or in part. These conditions and the events associated with them had to be specified before we could evaluate the appropriateness of future security alternatives. Thus, particular conditions are associated with specific phases or time periods, but not in a mechanistic or scheduled sense. It is important to keep this distinction in mind as we discuss each phase.

Phase One: The *Status Quo*

Phase One reflects prevailing circumstances. Under this situation, North and South Korea do not have a normal relationship. Neither is prepared to accord full legitimacy to its neighbor, although both recognize one another in *de facto* terms. However, even as confrontation and tension persist, the level of North Korean military threat is expected to decline. (This judgment assumes that North Korea's military capabilities will degrade further and that the ROK's defense capabilities will continue to improve.) But this phase is one of continued military threat, in which the potential for aggression by the North persists.

The *status quo* phase would continue until a process of peaceful coexistence began between South and North. The critical strategic breakpoint, therefore, would be actions that testified to movement away from a high level of political-military confrontation. Although there is a range of opinions among analysts on when this transition would be deemed under way, the two research teams agreed that the following conditions would need to be fulfilled:

- An appreciable redeployment of North Korea's offensively oriented military forces

- A full resolution of the status of the North Korean nuclear weapons program, including the verified disposal of North Korean plutonium and spent fuel that could be reprocessed into plutonium

- Elimination of North Korean reprocessing facilities

- Elimination of North Korea's chemical and biological weapons

- Activation of various mechanisms for a full-scale South-North dialogue.

Other events associated with movement away from the *status quo* would include the implementation of regular and special inspections by the International Atomic Energy Agency (IAEA), mutual South-North inspections, and activation of the Joint Nuclear Control Commission. We also anticipate the exchange of special envoys and hope for the completion of summit meetings between South and North. Should these steps be realized satisfactorily, they would pave the way for the full normalization of relations between the United States and North Korea and between Japan and North Korea.

Phase Two: Accommodation and Integration

In the accommodation and integration phase, peaceful coexistence would be fully established between North and South Korea, leading to the diminution and ultimate elimination of North Korea's military threat to the ROK. Official exchanges between relevant government ministries and heightened economic collaboration would be part of this process. Probable events during this phase would include the following:

- Implementation of confidence-building measures (CBMs) between the respective military establishments

- Completion of arms-reduction agreements between North and South Korea

- A preliminary agreement or understandings on an appropriate division of labor in military affairs.

We also anticipate that the basic and auxiliary agreements between South and North would be implemented, permanent missions exchanged, and the form and structure of a South-North confederation agreed on. This phase would also be associated with agreements on travel, communications, trade, and investment.

Phase Three: Post-Unification

Post-unification would be marked by a merger of North and South Korea, in which unified security and military policies would be implemented under a single sovereign entity and Korea would focus on countering potential regional instability and preventing the domination of the region by a single power. During this phase, a national military command authority and an integrated chain of command would also be established, with a single defense organization responsible for the nation's security. We also anticipate that Korea's aggregate force levels would be substantially reduced.

Our definition of peninsular characteristics leaves two central issues unaddressed. First, we have not specified how the transition process might unfold—in particular, whether movement toward unification is stimulated by instability and upheaval in the North or by step-by-step integration of the two Korean states. Second, we have not examined the larger regional setting (in particular, how regional states might adapt to future changes on the peninsula).

These analytic decisions reflect the major uncertainties that American and Korean policymakers confront in the coming decade. It is not realistic to identify all possible contingencies, let alone to prepare fully for each of them. We can, however, depict preferred outcomes and measure the effectiveness of various security alternatives either in realizing these outcomes or in mitigating the effects of developments disadvantageous to the interests of the United States and the ROK.

To pursue these issues further, we need to identify the factors that are most likely to shape decisionmaking in the future.

CRITERIA FOR EVALUATION

A central challenge for the two research teams was to define criteria for determining the appropriateness of different security approaches. This proved a complex task. Both teams needed to weigh where, when, and how Korean and American policy objectives and interests could differ and the potential significance of those differences. At the same time, the policy objectives under a given security alternative could readily exceed the resources that alliance partners are prepared to commit, or they could trigger adverse reactions from other regional states. Issues of clarity and specificity also arise: If an appropriate alliance bargain is to be struck between two or more countries, the understanding between leaderships must be reasonably straightforward and explicitly associated with mutually acceptable obligations and arrangements. These outcomes are easier to conceptualize in theory than they are to achieve in practice. But the prospects for devising a sustainable bargain will improve if the involved parties can specify their interests, commitments, and obligations in a reasonably explicit fashion. By contrast, without a clearly understood security compact, the United States and the ROK will have more difficulty restricting their areas of potential policy difference.

After extensive review, the two research teams reached agreement on three principal criteria by which to evaluate the respective interests and strategies of the two countries under different conditions and in relation to different possible alliance structures. In descending order of importance, the criteria were defined as follows:

- *Suitability:* How effective and relevant is a specific concept for meeting the vital security objectives and national interests of one or both countries?

- *Feasibility:* Can a given concept be put into practice and sustained at acceptable political and economic cost, and how viable is it likely to prove in relation to potential reactions from other states?

*   *Flexibility:* Can the concept adapt to unanticipated and even abrupt change in the prevailing assumptions underlying U.S. and ROK policy expectations and goals?

Each of these major criteria was further defined by ten subcriteria. These subcriteria are listed in Figures 4.1 through 4.3. Although most or all may seem self-explanatory, they reflect careful specification, refinement, and agreement between the two research teams. Each of the principal criteria also warrants elaboration.

Suitability

The goals encompassed under "suitability" concern the most important policy objectives shared by both states. They include goals that are especially prominent under the prevailing circumstances (for example, deterrence and defense against a North Korean attack, regional stability, and nonproliferation), but also goals whose significance would increase under conditions of peninsular change (for example, common economic prosperity, equitable defense burden-sharing, and democratic change). Nearly all these objectives,

RAND *MR594-4.1*

1. Deter/defend against North Korean attack

2. Prevent rise of regional hegemon

3. Maintain regional stability

4. Facilitate peaceful reunification

5. Foster ROK and U.S. economic prosperity

6. Protect overseas resources and lines of communication

7. Foster ROK self-sufficient defense capability

8. Counter nuclear proliferation

9. Achieve more-equitable burden-sharing

10. Foster democracy in region

Figure 4.1—Suitability Subcriteria

however, transcend the various peninsular phases discussed in this chapter. They constitute the irreducible set of goals to which the U.S.–ROK alliance is committed.

Feasibility

"Feasibility" concerns the domestic support in both states for pursuing shared alliance goals, and the capacity of both countries to pursue collaborative ends without incurring adverse effects from any of the ROK's neighbors. In essence, leaders in the United States and the ROK must be able to ensure that security cooperation rests on a strong and enduring consensus within each society. Without such a consensus, leaders will not be able to act decisively and self-confidently. These factors apply to the domestic publics of both countries: The citizens of any state must be persuaded that security obligations extended to an ally fulfill the objectives on which sovereignty and national interest ultimately depend—for example, guaranteeing a satisfactory voice in alliance decisionmaking, reducing the risks of military conflict, and enhancing the effectiveness of military forces at acceptable cost. Although the salience of a given consideration can increase under specific circumstances, the

RAND *MR594-4.2*

---

1. Maintain ROK independence and sovereignty

2. Fulfill international obligations (for example, U.S.–ROK treaty obligations)

3. Provide for major or equal influence in alliance decisionmaking

4. Diminish risks of a military conflict

5. Reduce each country's defense costs

6. Increase ROK–U.S. military effectiveness

7. Retain own forces under national command

8. Reduce political problems caused by presence of foreign troops in ROK

9. Generate domestic political support for alliance

10. Minimize potential negative effects on neighboring countries

---

Figure 4.2—Feasibility Subcriteria

broader set of concerns endures, and it does not attach exclusively to the beliefs of either the United States or the ROK.

Flexibility

The subcriteria shown in Figure 4.3 represent the value of security cooperation as an insurance policy. An alliance exists to enhance collaboration, but it also exists to deflect or to counter the effects of adverse outcomes, including those that are outside the purview of the specific alliance. The circumstances listed in the figure, therefore, are the outcomes that both countries most want to avoid—for example, a challenger state to the United States or a United States itself unwilling to fulfill its international obligations, internal instability in Northeast Asia, a severe deterioration of cooperation among the market economies of East Asia, or a failure in counterproliferation policy in the region. These are the major failures in policy that both countries hope to avoid but cannot preclude under all circumstances. The research teams sought to assess how well various security alternatives might function under this array of highly adverse circumstances.

RAND *MR594-4.3*

1. Respond to potential challenger to United States
2. Adapt to inward-looking United States
3. Insulate against internal unrest in China and/or Russia
4. Counter breakdown in U.S.–Japan relations
5. Counter breakdown in ROK–Japan relations
6. Counter collapse of regional cooperation
7. Counteract severe U.S.–ROK trade conflicts or heightened anti-Americanism in ROK
8. Provide insurance against potential adversaries other than DPRK
9. Protect against North Korean nuclear coercion
10. Respond to North Korean collapse

Figure 4.3—Flexibility Subcriteria

DISCUSSION OF RESEARCH FINDINGS

Alliances are dynamic rather than static entities. Even if particular national interests may be enduring, the specific factors shaping the terms of an alliance bargain can change and be redefined, especially in periods of major international realignment. To capture this complexity, the members of the two research teams were asked to evaluate the four principal security alternatives discussed in Chapter Three for the three separate peninsular phases, on the basis of the relevant criteria and subcriteria. (See Figure 4.4.) This assessment entailed completing nine separate matrices. On each matrix, the teams evaluated all four security alternatives for a specific phase-subcriterion combination. Individual scores from these evaluations furnished the basis for broader policy assessment. The team

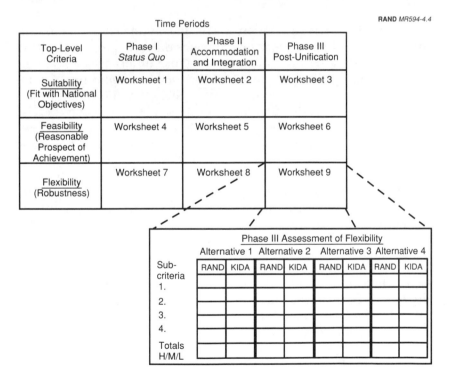

Figure 4.4—An Illustrative Assessment Matrix

members were asked to judge how the relevant policymaking bodies in both governments would be most likely to evaluate the adequacy and appropriateness of different security alternatives under shifting conditions. Each analyst was further asked to provide a score of high, medium, or low, characterizing the degree of fit between a specific alternative and the given subcriterion.

The raw scores were then tabulated and compared within and across both research teams. From their responses, the teams derived a convergent assessment, weighted according to the priority assigned to each of the major criteria (i.e., suitability was judged the most important, feasibility somewhat less important, and flexibility the least important). These final scores, however, are intended principally for illustrative purposes; the numbers should not be interpreted as being precise.

No two analysts agreed on every score. In certain cells of the matrix, individual members of the research teams differed quite markedly in their evaluations. In some instances, these differences appear attributable to the different meanings ascribed by various team members to particular subcriteria, so it is possible that the variation was not especially marked. But a major purpose of the research exercise was to see whether broad commonalities existed among the responses. Even acknowledging differences in interpretation and some variation in the overall scores, the areas of divergence do not seem to portend a major break in the alliance. Rather, both research teams appeared to coalesce around a set of preferred outcomes. Where there were differences in the assessments of the two teams, they were neither stark nor unbridgeable but, instead, offered valuable insights into the challenges of alliance management under conditions of change.

Given the complexity of the comparative assessment, we have not provided a detailed recapitulation of our findings. However, to enable readers to better grasp some of the principal judgments, we briefly highlight a few of the more important findings, drawing attention particularly to differences in the evaluations of the two teams and what might explain those differences. We first review our research results according to the three principal criteria, then shift to evaluations of the security alternatives, by phase.

Suitability

Neither team revealed marked disparities in judgment about suitability, especially under the *status quo* and the accommodation and integration phases. This convergence reflects the substantial overlap in the identified national interests of the two countries, as suggested in Chapter Two. (See Figures 2.1 and 2.2.) However, there is some divergence, and it reflects the U.S. position as a global power and the Republic of Korea's focus on peninsular concerns. For example, the RAND respondents judged a robust peninsular alliance as being of medium relevance to preventing regional hegemony or to protecting overseas resources and lines of communication under the *status quo* phase, whereas the KIDA respondents judged it to be of high relevance.

As consideration turned to the post-unification phase, some other differences emerged. Part of these differences seem attributable to longer-term unknowns, given that present relations are better understood than the hypothetical future implied by a post-unification alliance. In some instances, the KIDA respondents appeared relatively more sanguine about the capacity of looser security ties to achieve major policy goals. Although the differences were not stark, the findings suggest that future shifts in alliance concepts will require careful consultations and understandings between the two governments.

Feasibility

The RAND and KIDA scores differed most over the feasibility criterion. This comes as no surprise. As the two teams sought to characterize domestic views of the relationship, both revealed attentiveness to national sovereignty, decisionmaking roles within the alliance, perceptions of the distribution of the defense burden, and domestic sensitivities over command and control of military forces. Although these differences are not wholly consistent across security alternatives and peninsular phases, both teams see these differences as recurring issues.

The one exception to this judgment is under a regional security alliance, for which both research teams were strikingly uniform in their judgments, independent of the peninsular phase. This finding suggests that the relative salience of domestic concerns is likely to be less marked under circumstances in which both countries are involved in multinational security collaboration. Although seemingly paradoxical, this finding implies that an exclusive bilateral security relationship (particularly one with as much interdependence as the U.S.–ROK alliance) can magnify areas of divergence within domestic settings. Thus, expectations allies have of one another may be greater when no other security partners are involved.

These differences highlight how crucial the management of security cooperation is within a domestic context: The differences grew more marked as concerns about the immediacy of the North Korean threat diminished and as the separate domestic publics were more likely to voice increased sentiment for renegotiating the terms of the security relationship. For example, the desire of both leaderships (but especially the United States') for ensuring alliance effectiveness (including high degrees of interoperability in weapon systems) could come into conflict with the domestic desires in the ROK for enhancing Korea's decisionmaking autonomy. These desires include expectations that overall defense costs will be reduced, that the ROK's contributions to alliance burden-sharing will be reduced equivalently, and that the flow of U.S. defense technology to the ROK will be increased.

The RAND respondents, however, also characterized domestic attitudes in sharper terms, especially under the phases of diminished military threat: for example, greater U.S. priority on the cost-effectiveness of U.S. regional defense commitments and increasing U.S. concern with ensuring overall economic competitiveness. They also placed substantially greater importance on increasing responsibility-sharing on the part of regional allies such as the ROK, but within a framework that ensures a central U.S. political-security role.

These differences, however, do not suggest that alliance ties are irrelevant or outmoded. They do indicate clearly that the assumptions and relationships underlying security collaboration need to be rethought and refashioned as the security conditions, capabilities, and relative power of both countries undergo significant change. Without such an effort, domestic support for the alliance in both countries could decline, perhaps quite sharply—a consideration that warrants the attention of both leaderships.

Flexibility

The last of the three principal criteria exhibits the fewest differences in evaluation, especially under a robust security alliance. This finding does not seem surprising, given that the present relationship is the most interdependent and that the three other security alternatives posit appreciable adjustment in the combined capabilities of the two countries. The lack of divergence may suggest that both teams judge the possibility of a major breakdown in the principal political, economic, and security relationships in East Asia to be quite low. But it may also indicate the research analysts' difficulty in conceiving and weighing the implications of any severe regional crisis except various North Korean scenarios against which both countries prepare heavily. (It is only under the alternative of a political alliance that the teams believe response capabilities against a major North Korean crisis to be low.)

The major exception to this generally sanguine assessment concerns the future of the U.S. regional role. Both teams—but especially the RAND respondents—believe that under a reconfigured, regional, or political alliance, the capability of the U.S.–ROK relationship to counteract the negative effects of an inward-looking United States would diminish. The KIDA respondents appear less concerned about these possibilities than their RAND colleagues. But these divergent assessments may reflect different judgments on how either or both states might respond to major alterations in U.S. regional policy.

However, the purpose of this exercise was to weigh the implications for both countries of many varied futures, rather than to project or predict a specific event. It is only by assessing the consequences of future developments under shifting peninsular and regional conditions that we can evaluate the strengths and limitations of various security alternatives. To make these considerations more apparent, we need to briefly compare, by phase, the overall RAND and KIDA assessments of the four security alternatives.

1. A Robust Peninsular Alliance

During the *status quo* phase, a robust peninsular alliance received very high marks from both teams, especially according to the suitability and flexibility criteria. During the accommodation and integration phase, a robust peninsular alliance scored lower with both teams, especially on the decisive criterion of suitability. Both teams also doubted its feasibility in a domestic context, but the scores remained high with respect to flexibility: If major policy assumptions fail or are reversed, a robust alliance would continue to be able to adapt, although in some circumstances robustness might result in undue commitment to specific policies or relationships. In the post-unification phase, support for maintaining a robust alliance diminished even more sharply, especially among the KIDA respondents. Barring the development of a major new security threat to the Korean peninsula in this phase, it seems highly doubtful that this concept would remain readily sustainable for either country.

2. A Reconfigured Peninsular Alliance

A reconfigured alliance under *status quo* conditions was viewed warily by both teams, especially in relation to ensuring adequate deterrence and defense capabilities against a still-appreciable North Korean threat. Under the accommodation and integration phase, the scores improved for both teams. Both teams characterized this alternative as viable under a variety of future conditions, but not the preferred outcome, as compared with alternative security possibilities. Both teams, for example, showed particular concern about the adaptability and responsiveness of this alternative in the face of potential policy reversals, particularly if peninsular stability increases in the absence of the development of a viable regional security structure. Scores were comparable for the post-unification phase, although not particularly detrimental to either state. But if the region were characterized by increased rivalry, a reconfigured alliance could prove disadvantageous to the interests of both countries.

These findings suggest how the character of the regional security environment increasingly determines the policy calculations of the United States and the ROK once the peninsular threat diminishes. They also highlight that redefining, in parallel, regional security relationships is imperative for capitalizing on more-favorable peninsular conditions.

3. A Regional Security Alliance

Even under *status quo* conditions, a regional security alliance generates significant support. The RAND respondents were marginally more positive than KIDA's about its prospects. Under the accommodation and integration phase, RAND and KIDA both had an appreciably more favorable view of this concept. In the post-unification phase, positive support by both teams became more pronounced. Some KIDA respondents were skeptical about the feasibility of this alternative; however, KIDA's overall assessment was highly favorable: None of the team members proposed a low score for this concept in any of the three possible phases. But the major differences in various regional security models, discussed in Chapter Three, underscore the need to ensure that the concepts under review are clarified and precise.

4. A Political Alliance

Under *status quo* conditions, both research teams saw major risks in pursuing a political alliance, and their scores were congruent: A political alliance was not deemed acceptable according to any of the major criteria. The concept was deemed only marginally less objectionable and less risky in the accommodation and integration phase. In the post-unification phase, the risks to both countries generally persisted: A political alliance was seen as affording little flexibility should either country feel the need to reinvigorate security cooperation, although it performed somewhat better under the feasibility criterion, especially among the Korean respondents.

The aggregated scores in Figure 4.5 summarize and rank-order the preferences of the two teams. Under *status quo* conditions, both RAND and KIDA demonstrate a decided preference for a robust peninsular alliance. Under conditions of accommodation and integration, support shifts toward a regional security alliance, although the level of support is not as high as that associated with the robust peninsular alliance under the *status quo* phase. Support for a re-

Preferred Alternative, by Phase

RAND MR594-4.5

	Robust Peninsular Alliance		Reconfigured Peninsular Alliance		Regional Security Alliance		Political Alliance	
	KIDA	RAND	KIDA	RAND	KIDA	RAND	KIDA	RAND
Phase 1: *Status Quo*	1	1	3	3	2	2	4	4
Phase 2: Accommodation/ Integration	3	2	2	3	1	1	4	4
Phase 3: Post-Unification	4	3	2	2	1	1	3	4

NOTE: A "1" indicates highest rank.

Figure 4.5—Rank-Ordering the RAND and KIDA Assessments

gional security alliance is more pronounced under post-unification conditions. A reconfigured peninsular alliance also generates significant support, especially if a viable regional security structure emerges.

SUMMARY

For both teams, the relevance of a specific security alternative was determined predominantly by its capacity to address the vital national interests of the United States and Korea—underscoring the impossibility of designating a single optimal model for future U.S.–ROK security cooperation. Given that the definition of *national interest* under conditions of diminished threat shifts from a preoccupation with military security toward broader economic and political objectives, this conclusion seems especially germane.

However, the peninsular security environment remains the crucial consideration for the near- to mid-term future of the alliance. More than any other factor, it will determine perceptions of future needs and opportunities for both countries. Under existing conditions, a robust peninsular alliance remains relevant, especially given that North Korea may be entering a period of instability and major change. Should a process of accommodation and integration begin to take shape, it would be incumbent on the United States and the ROK to understand and explore the alternatives to present policy. Accommodation and integration presuppose important shifts in the security environment long prevalent on the peninsula. Under a diminished military threat, the two countries must show that they can manage areas of potential policy divergence.

To assess future options more fully, we turn our attention to *how* different security alternatives might develop and operate, and to gauging the larger implications of future security cooperation between the United States and Korea.

Chapter Five

EXAMINING TRANSITION PATHS TO THE NEXT CENTURY

The two research teams believe that there is a basis for sustaining security cooperation between the United States and Korea under a wide range of future conditions. Both teams concluded that maintaining or enhancing alliance relations conforms to the most important political and security interests of the two states, but that those relations must move from discussion of broad security alternatives to discussion of scope, breadth, and transition should major peninsular and regional change be under way: How can the security interests and goals of the two countries be maximized if the prevailing security circumstances begin to shift? What are the possible effects of changes in the existing alliance structure on ties between the United States and other U.S. regional security partners such as Japan? What are the potential responses of other regional actors? Finally, how do both countries proceed from here to there? What kinds of transition strategies and paths would be most beneficial and least disruptive to the interests of both countries? Put simply, how can the United States and Korea most effectively manage the dual transition in security cooperation—first, from decades of high threat to peninsular integration and, second, from integration to a more regionally based strategic concept?

OPERATIONAL COMPONENTS OF ALLIANCE RELATIONSHIPS

To explore these issues, we first need to review some of the main operational components that govern the U.S.–ROK alliance:

- A strategic concept that defines the shared obligations of alliance partners

- A common defense strategy through which roles, missions, and responsibilities are specified

- Agreement on the types and levels of forces required to implement a common defense strategy

- A range of more-specialized agreements on command relations, base arrangements, and burden-sharing.

In this chapter, we assess our security-cooperation alternatives and phases along some of these dimensions to highlight the complex interrelationships that will shape future deliberations.

END STATES AS DETERMINANTS OF TRANSITION PATHS

As discussed in Chapter Four, a robust peninsular alliance remains particularly relevant under conditions of an undiminished South-North confrontation. But a shift toward accommodation and integration would create different possible goals and directions, both for the mid-term and the longer term. We define these goals as the *end states* of the alliance. They represent the basic structure underlying security cooperation, and each potential end state represents different levels of integration and policy coordination. Equally important, the end state specifies how both countries propose to proceed from the existing security relationship to the future form of their alliance. Thus, definition of the preferred end state for the post-unification era would strongly dictate specific courses of action. The phase of accommodation and integration is transitional—in concept if not necessarily in duration—since it depends on the sustainability of the accommodation and integration process. Numerous analysts of Korean affairs argue that a reform-oriented North Korea could be maintained for an extended period of time (that is, for a decade or more), but others assert that moves toward political change would rapidly break down power and authority in the North, leading to abrupt reunification. On balance, however, few analysts posit an open-ended situation of separate, largely autonomous states.

Assuming movement toward unification, the two teams judged three security alternatives to be conceivable end states: (1) a reconfigured peninsular alliance; (2) one or another variant of a regional security alliance; or (3) a political alliance that assumes a largely autonomous Korea. For each end state, we assumed a transition process, or *path*, from the *status quo* phase to the post-unification phase. The process does not comprise a fixed sequence of events but does highlight critical policy concerns for both countries should the peninsular confrontation diminish or disappear.

In the judgment of the two teams, there are four principal paths for longer-term security cooperation between the United States and Korea. These paths are sketched in Figure 5.1. For each of the paths, we assumed that a robust peninsular alliance remains in place under *status quo* conditions. Beyond that point, however, the paths diverge. The first path posits a preferred post-unification end state of a reconfigured peninsular alliance, with a robust peninsular alliance remaining in place during the accommodation and integration phase. The second path posits a regional security alliance as the preferred end state, with a "mixed" peninsular-regional alliance

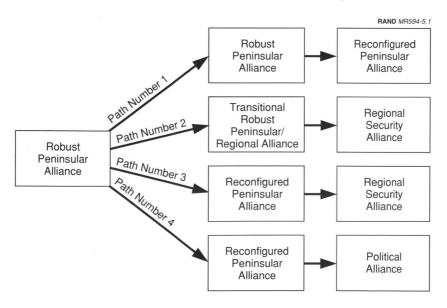

Figure 5.1—Four Principal Paths for Long-Term U.S.–Korean Security Cooperation

during the transition phase. The third path also posits a regional security alliance as the preferred end state, but argues for a reconfigured peninsular alliance as the security alternative during accommodation and integration. The fourth path envisions a political alliance as the preferred end state, with a reconfigured peninsular alliance serving as the security alternative during the transition. We now offer a preliminary assessment of the strengths and weaknesses of these different paths (diagrammed in Figures 5.2 through 5.5).

Path Number 1

The first path (Figure 5.2) has the obvious strength of maintaining a clear focus on peninsular security, enabling security objectives comparable to those maintained at present to be fulfilled. U.S. and ROK military roles and relationships would remain intact, but they might be adjusted periodically. By retaining substantial combined capabilities in the transition period, this orientation would leave both states well prepared for a variety of possible outcomes during the unification process, including some that might be destabilizing.

However, this approach also has shortcomings. It is lacking in flexibility, particularly if there are abrupt changes in the security environment during the accommodation and integration phase, which could introduce a sudden deterioration in the alliance relationship if the operational dimensions of U.S.–ROK security cooperation are overtaken by events.

Thus, a principal shortcoming would be that the pace of change might render existing institutional relations irrelevant to actual circumstances on the peninsula, possibly prompting domestic disaffection in the ROK with the workings of the alliance. By the same token, the United States would not want to be bound to an outmoded structure that no longer corresponds to peninsular realities. But these potential shortcomings should not be overemphasized: They become a source of concern only if events move rapidly and unexpectedly toward increased accommodation. Conversely, should authority break down abruptly in the North, the first path would give American and Korean decisionmakers substantial latitude in dealing with fast-moving events.

RAND *MR594-5.2*

	Phase 1: Robust Peninsular Alliance	Phase 2: Robust Peninsular Alliance	Phase 3: Reconfigured Peninsular Alliance
Strategic Concept	Combined defense of the Republic of Korea	⟶	Force reconstitution and crisis management
Military Relationships	U.S. leading/ Combined Forces Command system	⟶	Parallel command system established
U.S. Roles and Responsibilities	Support for forward defense; maritime security; outside reinforcement	⟶	Similar, but at lower levels
ROK Roles and Responsibilities	Ground combat and host-nation support (HNS)	⟶	Increased ground combat role; decreased HNS
Base System	Existing base system	⟶	Base closure/ realignment
Burden-Sharing	ROK maintains burden-sharing commitments	⟶	ROK decreases burden-sharing commitments as U.S. forces diminish

Figure 5.2—Path Number 1: Illustrative Dimensions

On balance, this path remains practicable so long as significant uncertainty persists in the peninsular security setting.

Path Number 2

The second path (Figure 5.3) permits substantial adaptability during the transition phase while achieving vital security objectives under conditions of uncertainty. It has the additional strength during the post-unification phase of enabling adaptation to a broad range of

RAND *MR594-5.3*

	Phase 1: Robust Peninsular Alliance	Phase 2: Transitional Robust Peninsular/Regional Alliance	Phase 3: Regional Security Alliance
Strategic Concept	Combined defense of the Republic of Korea	Primarily Korean defense, partly regional security	Korean defense and regional security paralleled
Military Relationships	U.S. leading/ Combined Forces Command system	Separate command; regional mission added	Separate command/wider regional command
U.S. Roles and Responsibilities	Support for forward defense; maritime security; outside reinforcement	80% robust peninsular focus, 20% regional focus	Power projection for regional conflicts; diminished peninsular role
ROK Roles and Responsibilities	Ground combat and host-nation support (HNS)	Increased ground combat role, limited regional orientation	Peninsular defense plus bases, access, and forces for regional roles
Base System	Existing base system	Partial base closure and adjustment	Base arrangements configured to regional requirements
Burden- Sharing	ROK maintains burden-sharing commitments	Burden-sharing commitments maintained; responsibility-sharing added	Burden-sharing commitments to depend on U.S. force presence; responsibility-sharing fully defined

Figure 5.3—Path Number 2: Illustrative Dimensions

longer-term security objectives by the United States and the ROK. However, the commitment during the transition phase to simultaneous pursuit of two security alternatives could result in differences between the alliance partners about the evolving roles of the two countries and about the force mix and structure of United States Forces, Korea (USFK). A very large premium would be placed on consultation and coordination during this interim period. Viewed in overall terms, the second path is a well-balanced approach that pays heed simultaneously to potential dangers and to longer-term opportunities.

Some of the largest challenges for the second path would be in reaching agreement on future-oriented alliance roles and responsibilities—not only for the United States and the ROK, but for the United States and other regional security partners. This path could also involve sensitivities on the part of China and Russia, both of whom would object strongly should an emerging regional alliance seem potentially directed against either of them. This concern highlights the importance of not configuring a regional security design against a specific threat. An additional challenge would be for Korea to more fully adapt to a new set of relations with Japan and other U.S. regional allies. We return to these issues in Chapter Six.

Path Number 3

The third path (Figure 5.4) exhibits important strengths for the ROK domestically, especially given the expected transfer of wartime operational control from a U.S. commander to a Korean commander. Under certain conditions, it would provide a means for an effective transition to a regional security structure, depending significantly on the overall power relationships within the region and on the character of U.S. relations with various major powers.

The transition to a reconfigured peninsular alliance might also afford promising avenues for improving South-North relations, if movement is away from high levels of confrontation. Its primary weakness would be the prospect of a rapid drawdown in USFK capabilities during the phase of accommodation and integration. Both the United States and the ROK would need to remain attentive to these transition issues, since overly rapid change could weaken their capabilities for effective response in a crisis.

However, this path is worthy of careful consideration, especially if a peninsular transition were fairly orderly. But it also runs some risk during the transition phase of generating uncertainty about the sustainability of the U.S. commitment to a longer-term regional role. This consideration highlights how critical it is for the United States to

RAND *MR594-5.4*

	Phase 1: Robust Peninsular Alliance	Phase 2: Reconfigured Peninsular Alliance	Phase 3: Regional Security Alliance
Strategic Concept	Combined defense of the Republic of Korea	Force reconstitution and crisis management	Korean defense and regional security paralleled
Military Relationships	U.S. leading/ Combined Forces Command system	Parallel command system established	Separate command/wider regional command
U.S. Roles and Responsibilities	Support for forward defense; maritime security; outside reinforcement	Similar, but at lower levels	Power projection for regional conflicts; diminished peninsular role
ROK Roles and Responsibilities	Ground combat and host-nation support (HNS)	Increased ground combat role, decreased HNS	Peninsular defense plus bases, access, and forces for regional roles
Base System	Existing base system	Base closure/ realignment	Base arrangements configured to regional requirements
Burden-Sharing	ROK maintains burden-sharing commitments	ROK decreases burden-sharing commitments as U.S. forces diminish	Burden-sharing commitments to depend on U.S. force presence; responsibility-sharing fully defined

Figure 5.4—Path Number 3: Illustrative Dimensions

clearly indicate its end-state goal during any peninsular drawdowns so that new security linkages could be established in the transition phase.

Path Number 4

The fourth path (Figure 5.5) has appeal for the domestic needs of both countries, reflecting, on the one hand, the desire of political forces within the ROK to enhance the country's self-defense

RAND *MR594-5.5*

	Phase 1: Robust Peninsular Alliance	Phase 2: Reconfigured Peninsular Alliance	Phase 3: Political Alliance
Strategic Concept	Combined defense of the Republic of Korea	Force reconstitution and crisis management	High-level political and security consultations
Military Relationships	U.S. leading/ Combined Forces Command system	Parallel command system established	Independent defense, wartime reinforcement
U.S. Roles and Responsibilities	Support for forward defense; maritime security; outside reinforcement	Similar, but at lower levels	Minimal presence, periodic exercises
ROK Roles and Responsibilities	Ground combat and host-nation support (HNS)	Increased ground combat role, decreased HNS	Near-total responsibility for defense of Korea
Base System	Existing base system	Base closure/ realignment	Comprehensive base realignment and closure
Burden-Sharing	ROK maintains burden-sharing commitments	ROK decreases burden-sharing commitments as U.S. forces diminish	No burden-sharing arrangements

Figure 5.5—Path Number 4: Illustrative Dimensions

responsibilities and, on the other hand, enabling budgetary savings for the United States. But such an approach would incur serious costs and risks for the U.S.–ROK combined defense strategy and could invite appreciable instability in the regional balance of power, also eroding the basis for future U.S.–ROK policy collaboration outside the national security arena. Such erosion could damage the interests of both countries, but those of the ROK in particular, because the ROK would have to pursue its future policy goals without a certain and clear commitment from the United States. Consequently, it is also likely that the United States would pursue options to enhance cooperation with other regional states to compensate for the diminished character of U.S.–ROK relations.

On balance, for the long-term interest of the two countries, the fourth path appears the least appropriate of the four approaches, because it would have wider reverberations for overall U.S.–ROK relations.

SUMMARY

This evaluation underscores the interconnectedness of alliance relations at both a strategic level and an operational level. Redesigning alliances is not only a question of new concepts and policies, but of the underlying commitments, expectations, and assumptions of the partners. Ensuring satisfactory security cooperation under uncertain circumstances and with many potential paths places great demands on the political resources of alliance partners and will require judicious policy management both domestically and internationally—especially when an alliance's strategic orientation and operational dimensions have endured for so long, and where the character of the threat has been clearly perceived and understood for decades. But the possible transitions facing both countries reflect the potential for change in the U.S.–ROK security policy environment.

To consider further how both countries might best deal with these possible transition challenges, we need to place the future of the alliance in the context of the threats, dangers, and opportunities the United States and the Republic of Korea are likely to confront over the next decade.

Chapter Six

CONCLUSIONS AND RECOMMENDATIONS FOR POLICY

In this concluding chapter, we step back from the joint research findings and examine some of the larger policy concerns that the United States and the Republic of Korea appear likely to face in the coming ten years. Despite its major accomplishments, the U.S.–ROK alliance now confronts the profound challenges of redefinition and transition, for which history offers only limited guidance. Although both countries continue to attach great importance to security cooperation, their record of collaboration and interdependence may not suffice to sustain close cooperation should the North Korean threat diminish appreciably or should unification take place. Likewise, without appropriate regard for higher-level strategic concerns during a transition period, security cooperation could prove more contentious within both countries or become mired in lesser policy disputes. To sustain their security relationship over the longer term, both the United States and the Republic of Korea must, therefore, mutually recognize and pursue future-oriented common interests, effectively articulate these interests within their societies, and implement policy goals that flow from those interests.

Both study teams view their findings as demonstrating the value and benefits that would accrue to the two countries by sustaining security cooperation over the longer term. By reinvigorating such ties, both states will be more likely to secure their respective vital interests, and the region as a whole will be more stable. By contrast, for either country or both to devote insufficient attention to alliance renewal would very likely undermine the broader basis of Korean-

American collaboration and weaken the security position of both states in Northeast Asia.

We therefore need to view the necessity for alliance redefinition and/or transition according to three principal dimensions: (1) the threats and dangers that the Republic of Korea and the United States jointly face at present; (2) over-the-horizon opportunities that could be pursued to mutual advantage; and (3) the respective contributions that the two countries might make to a future-oriented alliance.

THREATS AND DANGERS

The largest threats to regional peace and stability are still posed by a vulnerable and potentially volatile North Korea. The United States, the Republic of Korea, and other regional states look forward to the day when leaders in the North recognize that political and economic openness represent guiding principles for the Asia of the twenty-first century. But we cannot assume the inevitability of peaceful, orderly movement toward such an outcome. To this point, the successor leadership to Kim Il Sung has been neither able nor willing to confront issues of political and economic change, leaving North Korea frozen in time.

Many observers believe that a measure of policy change is portended by the signing of the U.S.–North Korea Agreed Framework in October 1994 and the June 1995 agreement on provision of replacement nuclear reactors under the auspices of the Korean Peninsula Energy Development Organization (KEDO). But it is far too soon to make definitive judgments. If North Korea envisions the Agreed Framework and the KEDO program primarily as means to undermine the U.S.–ROK alliance or as a way to buy time to realize unfulfilled ambitions in weapons development, then both sets of negotiations with North Korea are doomed to ultimate failure. The United States and the ROK retain shared incentives to ensure North Korea's compliance with its obligations under the Nuclear Nonproliferation Treaty and the Joint Declaration of the Denuclearization of the Korean Peninsula. These goals will be realized only through determined, persistent efforts to hold North Korea to its obligations. Pending realization of these policy objectives, both countries need to move with prudence and care in their dealings with the North.

The nuclear issue, however, is symptomatic of an even larger issue: the survival of the North Korean regime. At present, Kim Il Sung's death and the leadership uncertainties that have attended his passing have increased the possibility of abrupt and destabilizing change on the peninsula. North Korea continues to fiercely resist measures that could help stabilize the South-North relationship. It seeks to deal separately and exclusively with the United States, thereby hoping to undermine the U.S.–ROK relationship. Even in the face of extreme economic deprivation, the North remains unwilling to pursue fuller economic ties with the ROK, since the leadership fears that such contact and cooperation could undermine its absolute grasp on political power, putting the future of the North Korean system at risk.

It is not possible to specify the circumstances under which the North Korean leadership would be prepared to undertake meaningful change in South-North relations. For example, North Korea may view the Agreed Framework principally as a means to garner the economic assistance that is indispensable to its continued existence, but with Pyongyang having little intention to pursue more-stable, normalized relations with the ROK. This possibility in no way invalidates the need for prudent efforts to engage Pyongyang, in particular through a vigorous activation of the South-North negotiation process. But such measures presume that North Korea is ready to take relations with the ROK seriously and is willing to accept the ROK's legitimacy as a sovereign state. They also presume that North Korea is ready to undertake significant steps to decrease the very high levels of military tension and confrontation between the two Koreas and to enable full verification of such change. However, North Korea's accelerated efforts to undermine the armistice agreements inspire little confidence that leaders in the North have turned a corner or that they are prepared to make a decisive break with their past policies of confrontation and military threat.

Both the United States and the Republic of Korea need to impart unambiguously to North Korea that their security cooperation is not a negotiable item in any accommodation process with the North. Only then can both countries hope that leaders in Pyongyang might reassess their past policies, forgo destabilizing weapon-acquisition programs, and seek a meaningful accommodation with the South. Therefore, a vigorous, active security relationship between the United States and the Republic of Korea remains an essential component of a larger strategy of inducing change in the North. Negotiations with Pyongyang do not invalidate the necessity of continued preparations against threats still posed by the North—threats that involve more than the canonical North Korean threat across the 38th Parallel. North Korea's internal vulnerabilities might also create contingencies that the U.S.–ROK alliance must understand and address as fully as possible. Thus, the two countries should not passively await the onset of change in the North or simply assume that past threats will disappear uneventfully from the scene. Both countries need to face such challenges together, because the prospect of abrupt change in the North entails serious risks to the interests of the ROK, the United States, and Northeast Asia as a whole. The increased potential for instability in the North makes a strengthened U.S.–ROK consultative process crucial for managing any future crisis on the peninsula.

A range of prospective scenarios in future relations between North and South Korea, each with important implications for the day-to-day conduct of U.S.–ROK security relations, presents itself. Defense planning between the United States and South Korea is still focused primarily on deterring and defeating a major conventional assault from the North. Given that the deployment of North Korean forces remains unchanged at present, there is every reason to maintain deterrence and defense at a robust level. But the future may offer a more complex scenario to which the U.S. and ROK defense establishments would need to adapt. In broad terms, five principal scenarios seem possible:

- North Korea remains defiant toward the ROK, with high levels of military confrontation sustained indefinitely, possibly augmented by ballistic missile deployments

- A step-by-step internal transition in the North permits accommodation to be initiated (perhaps beginning with economic integration) between the two Koreas

- A more mixed picture, wherein North Korea pursues relations with the ROK on a fitful, inconsistent basis (for example, signals of accommodation are interspersed with continued coercive threats and lingering uncertainties about the North's nuclear program)

- Abrupt internal changes in the North, not excluding internal collapse and rapid movement toward unification

- A decision by North Korea (possibly induced by a belief that time is not on its side) to launch hostilities against the ROK.

Although it is impossible to predict with confidence the most likely path of future developments, the United States and the ROK have a compelling need to closely coordinate their efforts in any of the above circumstances. At the same time, they have an equal need to ensure that North Korea does not inject itself into the workings of the alliance (for example, by seeking to undermine U.S.–ROK political and security ties as a condition for advancing its relations with the United States). Thus, if it proves feasible to open simultaneous channels between the United States and North Korea and between South and North, these respective relationships must be pursued so that they support rather than undermine U.S. and ROK long-term goals for the peninsula—that is, a Korea that moves toward unification free from coercion or threat, that is truly free of nuclear weapons, that remains amenable to continued cooperation with the United States, and that is closely identified with the community of market-oriented democracies.

However, because of increased risks of instability and the potential for abrupt change in the North, U.S. and ROK contingency planning must also carefully consider military actions that North Korea might undertake, especially if its circumstances appear increasingly desperate. This need remains crucial so long as the United States and the Republic of Korea confront a hostile, threatening North Korean state.

FUTURE OPPORTUNITIES

Even as the Republic of Korea and the United States enhance their planning and consultative arrangements over the near- to mid-term, they have a parallel need to broaden their vision of security cooperation beyond the peninsula. U.S. forces in Korea have long served broader regional goals, especially that of reinforcing the U.S. commitment to a stable balance of power in Northeast Asia. Should the North Korean threat lose its relevance as a central organizing concept for the alliance and for U.S. deployments in Northeast Asia, the logic of security cooperation would necessarily undergo a major change. Some analysts, for example, would then posit a more benign security environment. This belief would, in turn, argue for a reduction of U.S. forces deployed in the Western Pacific and diminished institutional and operational relationships between the United States and various regional security partners. But this judgment assumes that alliance structures *must* be tied to a specific definition of military threat.

To the contrary, alliances do not necessarily require a central, organizing threat to maintain their relevance. They can serve as integrative institutions through which more-inclusive political and economic mechanisms will develop and states will be more able to limit areas of potential policy divergence outside the national security realm. Alliances also provide a means whereby states can commit military capabilities of a more generic nature, which seems especially appropriate in relation to the complexities and uncertainties of post–Cold War Asia. Continued security collaboration, therefore, remains a prudent means of preparing for potential crises and for lesser adverse policy developments that could transpire in the future.

Seen in this light, a renewed alliance would provide a transition between present dangers to a future that affords genuine promise, but in which the uncertainties also remain great. It would constitute an indispensable means for the United States to sustain interaction, communication, and collaboration in a region of abiding American interest. At the same time, it would help ensure that the Republic of Korea pursues its longer-term goals with full attention to the requirements of regional stability and to how its own interests can best be ensured within a framework of continued security cooperation with the United States.

In Northeast Asia, a regional security structure would help provide the underpinning for longer-term well-being, prosperity, and stability, on all of which the interests of the United States and its regional partners will continue to depend. Although this structure would ideally involve all regional states, such inclusion is likely to prove a long-term goal rather than a viable objective in the near- to mid-term. In the absence of domestic transitions that would permit a viable multilateral security regime to be created in Northeast Asia, the United States and its principal security partners have clear incentives to build on their record of success by sustaining close coordination and interoperability of forces—a prerequisite to more-inclusive relationships that might ultimately develop regionwide.

Even these interim measures, however, would entail forming structures and relationships very different from those maintained during the Cold War. Unlike in Europe, U.S. security involvement in Northeast Asia has been predominantly bilateral rather than multilateral. Consequently, moves toward a regional security structure in Northeast Asia presuppose much more active collaboration and coordination not only between the United States and its regional partners, but also among the regional states themselves. Even though the United States needs to reiterate its continued commitment to the ROK's well-being and security, its obligations would be shaped by a larger set of U.S. security requirements, in which the ROK and other states (most notably, Japan) would assume roles and responsibilities commensurate with their capabilities and national interests. Under such circumstances, the United States would no longer define its regional presence and commitments predominantly in bilateral terms: regional security planning would involve the whole, rather than the sum of its parts.

Moves toward a more regionally based defense concept would undoubtedly require that the United States carefully consult with and understand the concerns of its regional security partners. The Republic of Korea and Japan in particular have long been accustomed to security ties with the United States that are highly exclusive and do not require them to interact extensively with other U.S. security partners. However, future U.S. defense requirements—especially if the United States should move toward a regionally based alliance concept—would be more generic and would place increased emphasis on flexibility and cost-effectiveness, as well as involving much larger efforts to ensure integration and communication between and among America's current regional security partners, thereby avoiding needless duplication and redundancy in command arrangements, operational procedures, and U.S. forward deployments.

Any transition to a fully developed regional concept and security structure will necessarily be incremental. All major powers would need to be consulted in this process so that recommended changes could be initiated and implemented with full preparation, not undertaken in the face of determined opposition by one or more regional states. And, given that each of America's regional security partners has long been accustomed to a predominantly bilateral defense relationship with the United States, it will be incumbent on the United States to endorse this process of change. But a gradualist approach would seem relevant both to recognize Korean domestic sensitivities (for example, in relation to future ties with Japan) and to minimize the possibilities of adverse reactions from any of the ROK's neighbors, especially China.

Thus, just as the Korean War helped define the security framework in Northeast Asia over the past 45 years, Korean unification could have an equally significant effect on the structure of regional security in the twenty-first century. The challenge for the United States and the ROK would be to define a logic and structure for a post-unification alliance that enables both countries to sustain cooperation once the North Korean threat ceases to exist. But a future-oriented strategy will require that both countries make major adjustments in how they think about security cooperation. Although it is impossible to be precise about the specific dimensions of such collaboration, it is not too early to begin discussing some of its possible goals and directions.

TOWARD A NEW STRATEGIC CONCEPT

A future-oriented alliance explicitly assumes a credible strategic concept and a set of mutual obligations for fulfilling such a concept. Given the present uncertainties on the peninsula and in the region as a whole, we have tried to illustrate some of these possibilities rather than to specify a preferred course of action relevant in all contexts. But it is necessary at this point to identify some operative principles and the implications and understandings that could flow from them.

A Profit-Generating Alliance

Figure 6.1 presents a proposed rationale for the future of the alliance. It reminds both countries that, whereas a threat-based rationale very effectively served the interests of the United States and the ROK during the Cold War, the challenges of the future will be very differ-

RAND *MR594-6.1*

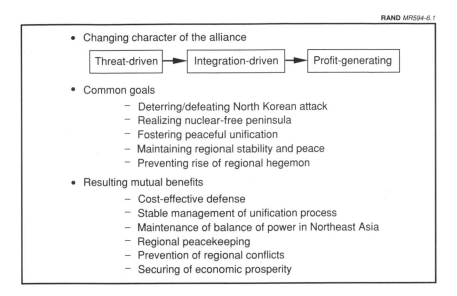

- Changing character of the alliance

  | Threat-driven | ➤ | Integration-driven | ➤ | Profit-generating |

- Common goals
  - Deterring/defeating North Korean attack
  - Realizing nuclear-free peninsula
  - Fostering peaceful unification
  - Maintaining regional stability and peace
  - Preventing rise of regional hegemon
- Resulting mutual benefits
  - Cost-effective defense
  - Stable management of unification process
  - Maintenance of balance of power in Northeast Asia
  - Regional peacekeeping
  - Prevention of regional conflicts
  - Securing of economic prosperity

Figure 6.1—Strategic Rationale for a Continued U.S.–ROK Security Alliance

ent. During a highly delicate transition period, a new alliance concept must guarantee peninsular stability while seeking to foster integration between North and South Korea. In its fully developed form, the concept must demonstrate why and how the United States and the Republic of Korea will benefit much more fully by continued close cooperation than by pursuing independent paths. A future alliance concept also must be undertaken in a manner that does not pose serious risks to the interests of other regional actors.

The two teams have described this approach as a "profit-generating" alliance. We do not mean *profit* in a strictly economic sense, although we believe that a renewed alliance would serve the economic interests of both states. Rather, such an alliance could serve a broad spectrum of mutual interests, and such interests would be much more fully enhanced if both countries maintain a highly interactive and collaborative security relationship than if they do not. The alliance would serve common goals during all three phases of security cooperation (that is, the period of continued North Korean threat, the period of South-North integration, and the post-unification era).

The outcomes generated by this cooperation would then bring added value in relation to both countries' security needs, at more reasonable cost to both. Equally important, the resulting benefits would not confer unilateral advantage on either security partner; both would gain equally from them.

Alliance Benefits

A future-oriented alliance realizes the following benefits:

- Peninsular security would be achieved at more acceptable cost to both states.

- The unification process would be more effectively managed with less possibility of costly, highly disruptive outcomes.

- There would be increased assurance of regional stability and security, including a lower likelihood of regional military conflict.

- More-developed regional peacekeeping capabilities would be constituted, and both states as well as other regional actors could participate.

- Both states would have increased incentives to foster mutually beneficial economic policies.

Without the commitment to build a new alliance, all these goals could be undermined—or imperiled outright.

These benefits convey how a broad spectrum of political, economic, and security gains could be realized by building a longer-term strategic partnership between the United States and a unified Korea. Equally important, these benefits would be secured at less cost to both countries than under separate pursuit of independent strategies, in a manner that benefited their respective interests. A new alliance would presuppose continued security interdependence, with both countries bringing distinct capabilities and contributions to the partnership. As a global power, the United States would furnish power-projection capabilities that could be placed in the service of shared security interests. But the United States is seeking reliable, long-term partners in its efforts to ensure global and regional stability; it cannot undertake these missions unilaterally.

The Republic of Korea is a logical and appropriate partner for many reasons:

- It has a long record of close cooperation with U.S. military forces.

- Its military personnel are well-trained and highly skilled.

- It explicitly seeks to maintain security cooperation with the United States in the post-unification era.

- Korea will be increasingly able (in conjunction with the United States) to serve as a net exporter of security rather than an importer. Working in close collaboration with the United States, Korea would help augment security rather than rely heavily on the United States to provide it.

For these reasons, the two countries would be able to coordinate their respective national policies toward a larger shared end: the prevention of conditions that could lead to future instability or to another state's seeking predominance in a region of vital interest to both Korea and the United States.

Alliance Challenges

These broad objectives, however, constitute only the first steps in a process of building a sustainable, longer-term security consensus between the United States and the ROK. The two research teams in no way minimize the major challenges that would be encountered in moving the alliance from its present form to a successor version. To fulfill its potential, a new alliance concept for the next century will require careful planning, development, and endorsement by both countries. It will also require extensive discussion and coordination with other regional actors and with other U.S. security partners, especially Japan. The United States seeks to maintain close security relations with both Korea and Japan. Any future transition in U.S.–ROK security relations should not be made at the expense of U.S.–Japanese security ties, but should seek means to further strengthen them.

Some of the crucial questions to be raised in such discussions, for example, will involve the future apportionment of roles, responsibilities, and relationships between U.S. and ROK forces, and the relationship of the operational procedures between the two countries and those involving other U.S. security partners. This project did not explore in detail the types of security institutions that might be most relevant to a future-oriented alliance, nor did it assess the precise missions, force postures, and doctrines that would be most appropriate in a post-unification context. For the present, we note just briefly some of the issues that will require careful exploration by both governments.

Issues for Both Governments

The central consideration affecting a future alliance will be how tasks will be divided among the United States, Korea, and other prospective contributors to a regional security structure. Decisions on a division of tasks would be based directly on issues of cost, commitment, force deployments, and the range of responsibilities these forces might fulfill. Our focus here will be limited to some of the key issues that the United States and Korea would need to consider.

As noted in Chapter Three, a regional security alliance would comprise diverse considerations. The precise forms of security collaboration would depend on the comparative advantage that each country would bring to such an alliance. For example, the United States has clear strengths in power projection, intelligence assets, and the application of new information and communication technologies to various defense needs. As well, in some contexts the forward presence of U.S. forces would remain crucial, with the ROK able to provide the requisite base structure and needed facilities for the prepositioning of equipment and associated logistics requirements. Over time, we would expect a clear focus (through combined exercises, officer exchanges, and information-sharing) on ensuring interoperability of U.S. and Korean forces, and for both countries to commit specialized forces to particular roles and responsibilities, depending on cost, need, and the mix of combined and joint defense activities.

All these considerations would affect the scope and character of the future U.S. military presence on the peninsula. The post–unification security environment would appreciably change the U.S. force mix. For example, the United States might decide to focus on maintaining more-generic capabilities in Korea to address a broad set of potential needs and contingencies. Remaining U.S. forces on the peninsula would need to be restructured to fit new military requirements, with an increased emphasis on mobility. New deployments, such as the possible basing of U.S. naval assets in Korea, would reflect the different requirements imposed by a regional security arrangement. These decisions, in turn, would centrally affect future Korean roles and security responsibilities.

A STATEMENT OF SECURITY EXPECTATIONS

In essence, the United States and the Republic of Korea need to devise a mutually acceptable statement of security expectations and needs for the longer term—a statement, or contract, that would build on earlier successes, but in a manner reflecting very different security challenges. Both research teams believe that there would be ample value to both countries in building a post-unification alliance. In their logic, however, the two countries would need to move beyond security cooperation based on a specific military threat.

The redesigning of the Korean-American alliance will not happen automatically or easily. Development of future security alternatives requires the close attention of both leaderships as well as careful attention to the implications of the alternatives for the region as a whole. Efforts must be begun now to look to the day when a unified Korea can assume its rightful place as a leading actor in a regional security system for Asia and the Pacific and identify a preferred path to beneficial end states for the future. It will be incumbent on both the United States and the Republic of Korea to weigh carefully and systematically the requirements of security cooperation in the face of dynamic change, existing dangers and risks, and potential opportunities. At the same time, a more ambitious concept for the future requires ample understanding and domestic support within both countries and due regard for regional realities.

The results of this research demonstrate the value of developing an alliance strategy for the longer term. It is incumbent on both the United States and the Republic of Korea to fashion these opportunities and possibilities in a manner that benefits not only the two countries but Asia and the Pacific as a whole. Viewed in this larger perspective, now is the time to begin to plan for the next century.